PRAISE FOR
LORD, I KEEP GETTING A BUSY SIGNAL

Thank God for this honest, down-to-earth, confessional book about prayer, Bible study, and finding the Christian way. It's a book for which many people have been waiting, most of them probably without knowing it. Readers will identify with it so naturally and completely that when they have finished reading it they will possess the equivalent of a lifetime graduate degree in its subjects.

The little stories and quotations alone are worth far more than the price of the book. So buy it, read it, and, above all, practice it. Your whole life will be different for having done so.

John Killinger
former pastor, and professor at Vanderbilt, Chicago, Princeton and Samford University, and the author of many books including *Beginning Prayer* and *God's People at Prayer.*

A wise and searching reflection by a superlative pastor and theologian on life centered around prayer as the definitive activity of Christian faith. Impressively grounded in scriptures, theology, and experience, *Lord, I Keep Getting a Busy Signal* will stretch your mind, touch your heart, and intensify your desire to give God first place in your life.

E. Glenn Hinson
Emeritus Professor of Spirituality and John Loftis Professor of Church History, Baptist Theological Seminary at Richmond

There are a myriad of books that speak to the spiritual life. Many offer short cuts, but because Bill Tuck has years of pastoral experience he has come to understand that there are no short cuts. Emerging from that experience as a pastor of many years, Bill writes with wisdom and grace, offering us an extremely helpful guide to overcoming the barriers we put up to allowing God's Spirit room to work in our lives.

Dr. Robert Cornwall
Pastor, Central Woodward Christian Church
(Disciples of Christ)
Editor, Sharing the Practice (Academy of Parish Clergy)
Author of several books, including: *Unfettered Spirit: Spiritual Gifts for the New Great Awakening* (Energion, 2013)

OTHER BOOKS BY
WILLIAM POWELL TUCK

The Journey to the Undiscovered Country: What's Beyond Death?

A Pastor Preaching: Toward a Theology of the Proclaimed Word

The Pulpit Ministry of the Pastors of River Road Church, Baptist (Editor)

The Last Words from the Cross

Overcoming Sermon Block (APC)

LORD, I KEEP GETTING A BUSY SIGNAL

REACHING FOR A BETTER SPIRITUAL CONNECTION

WILLIAM POWELL TUCK

Energion Publications
Gonzalez, FL
2014

Some Scripture quotations are from the Revised Standard Version of the Bible (RSV), copyright 1946, 1952 © 1971, 1973, by the Division of Christian Education of the National Council of Churches of Christ in the USA.

Some Scripture quotations are from the New Revised Standard Version of the Bible (NRSV), copyright © 1989 by the Division of the Christian Education of the National Council of the Churches of Christ in the USA.

Some Scripture quotations are from the King James Version of the Bible (KJV), in the public domain.

Some Scripture quotations are from The New English Bible (NEB). Copyright © the Delegates of the Oxford University Press and the Syndics of the Cambridge University Press, 1961, 1970.

Some Scriptures are the author's translations.

Cover Image from Dreamstime, ID #1711902 © Rossco | Dreamstime.com

Cover Design: Henry E. Neufeld

ISBN10: 1-63199-004-7
ISBN13: 978-1-63199-004-5
Library of Congress Control Number: 2014934811

Energion Publications
P. O. Box 841
Gonzalez, FL 32560

850-525-3916
energion.com
pubs@energion.com

In memory of Catherine Maddox Campbell
Who first introduced Emily, her daughter, and my wife,
to the significance of prayer

TABLE OF CONTENTS

PREFACE

Throughout my life I have sought to commune with God. I have undertaken this endeavor in many places. I have found moments of contemplation in —

quiet, small, white-framed country churches, in large traditional or contemporary-designed urban churches, in ancient Gothic cathedrals in Europe, in a Quaker Meeting House, and in tent meetings,

by lakes, rivers, creeks or sea shores,

on secluded wooden mountainsides, on top of an extinct volcano, on white and black sand beaches, by campfires at night,

before a blazing fire in my own den, in my study, on park benches,

walking through multicolored hillsides in the fall,

pausing beside a snow blanketed field, beside waterfalls,

jogging along roadsides,

following the path of saints from the past, secluding myself from others,

fasting,

finding an oasis of quiet in a noisy city and immersing myself in its stillness, and in many other ways.

In many and varied modes, I have looked for ways to meditate. I have seldom found this desire so easily met or the place and conditions ideal. I have often been embarrassed to admit that praying has not come so easily or naturally to me.

I thought for a long time that this was simply a reflection on my personality or background. I soon discovered, however, in my

Christian pilgrimage that most persons I know struggled with the same difficulty. Too many laypersons were content to have their pastor do their praying for them on Sunday morning. Prayer was not their "thing." In our busy, modern world, prayer seems so remote, old-fashioned, and impractical. "Leave prayer to the professional holy men and women. We have real work to do," they say.

Yet, I have heard ministers complain because laypersons interrupt their time for praying and give them so much busy work that they have little time to pray. One minister I know got in trouble with his church because he refused to give up the time he had set aside for prayer to attend a denominational breakfast meeting. He considered his prayer time so important that he would not let anything change it, even a denominational church meeting.

On the other hand, I have heard lay persons express dismay that their minister was not a praying person and refused to offer them any spiritual guidance. I have also known many devoted ministers and laypersons who have longed to deepen their spiritual life. My spiritual life has been enriched by both laypersons and ministers. I know one layman who arises each morning at 5:30 a. m. and prays and meditates for an hour. He has continued this practice for twenty-five years. I know a minister who sets aside several hours a day for quiet reflection. Are these persons exceptions? I am afraid they are.

I am convinced that one reason more laypersons and ministers do not spend more time in meditation is not because these persons do not love God or the Christ-like way, but they lack spiritual discipline to aid them in their religious journey. This little book is one pilgrim's suggestions on what has been meaningful to him. I have not tried to offer more than a brief sketch to throw some light on the path. I do not believe that our habits of superficial prayer time will ever change until we take seriously the necessity for spiritual disciplines.

During part of the writing of these pages, I secluded myself in a retreat setting at the Abbey of Gethsemani near Bardstown,

Kentucky. Here in this Trappist monastery, established in 1848 and dedicated to prayer, silence and labor, I went apart to learn from those who take prayer so seriously that they have devoted their lives to it. Observing these monks as they chant their psalms and prayers to God and silently go about their daily tasks has been a real lesson in spiritual values for me. I realize that I, who claim to be a spiritual leader, have not taken the power of prayer seriously enough and feel ashamed of my devotion to God measured by these men. Their devotion to discipline inspires me to a more meaningful discipline of my own. The road lies before me and you. We can choose the easy, superficial way or the higher path of meaningful, deep meditation and prayer. The most famous of the Trappist monks, Thomas Merton, has observed:

The fact remains that contemplation will not be given to those who willfully remain at a distance from God, who confine their interior life to a few routine exercises of piety and a few external acts of worship and service performed as a matter of duty. . . God is only invited to enter this charmed circle to smooth out difficulties and to dispense rewards.[1]

If you and I are going to experience more than a "nod" to God in our devotional life, then a genuine commitment has to be made to spiritual solitude and meditation. If the real purpose of the contemplative life is to be in union with God in our desires and goals, then prayer cannot be confined to the marginal and secondary areas of our life. Contemplation—to think the thoughts of God after God—will not be achieved by careless, lazy or infrequent methods. A depth of discipline will be required. There can be no greater joy than the knowledge that "I am in God and God is in me."

Several of these chapters were presented as a part of the Offterdinger-Williamson Preaching & Lecture Series at the First Presbyterian Church in Lynchburg, Virginia. I appreciate their gracious response to the presentations. I want to express my ap-

---

1   Thomas Merton, *What Is Contemplation?* (Springfield, Illinois: Templegate Publishers, 1978), 12.

preciation to Carolyn Stice, my secretary at St Matthews Baptist Church in Louisville, Kentucky for ten years, for typing this manuscript through several drafts. She always acted like it was no real effort when I knew otherwise. I also want to express my thanks to Sandra Bundick, the former Administrative Assistant at Hampton Baptist Church in Hampton, Virginia where I had the privilege of serving, for getting the manuscript in final form. The labor of both of these persons is greatly appreciated.

I send this small volume out with the prayer that others will be enriched in their contemplative life by it.

CHAPTER 1

"LORD, I KEEP GETTING A BUSY SIGNAL"

To be very frank, I have to tell you that it has never been easy for me to understand people for whom praying comes easily. It has always been a struggle for me. It has been a struggle to find the time, to keep the time, to make it meaningful, to avoid interruption, and to sense the reality of the presence of God always in my prayer time. There are some people who make me very uncomfortable with their concept of prayer. To me, their God seems a bit like a bellhop. You simply give him your wish and God is supposed to do it. To some, prayer is like a rabbit's foot or a luck charm. You "carry" it with you in case you get in some kind of trouble and then you pray. Prayer for others is a kind of Aladdin's Lamp. You rub it and your wishes are instantly satisfied. People like this make me very uncomfortable with their understanding of prayer.

Then there are others who know something about struggle in praying. They have prayed to God, lifted up their voices toward heaven, but heaven seemed to be made of brass. They have voiced their wishes to God, their needs to God, their hopes to God, their aspirations to God, and yet they keep getting a busy signal. "Lord," they say, "I pray, but I only get a busy signal." Their prayers seem to go unanswered. A mother whose son was a soldier in Iraq prayed that her son would come home safely. But he was killed along with several other soldiers by a suicide bomber. During the Second World War, a group of Christians gathered in church and prayed that they might be safe from the Nazi bombings. Even in the midst of their praying, bombs fell on the church and they were all killed. C. S. Lewis, after the death of his wife, raised the question in *A Grief Observed*: Where is God when your need is desperate? He responded to his own question about what one often finds. "A door slammed in your face, and the sound of bolting and double bolting on the inside. After that silence."[2]

Many prayed that Hurricane Katrina would miss their houses, but their section of the Gulf Coast was devastated. Some people have prayed for good health, but all of their lives they have been plagued with bad health. There are some farmers who pray to God for rain, but rain doesn't fall for months. And others who pray that it will stop raining, and yet floods come. A minister related an experience he had when he discovered his nine year old daughter had leukemia. He came into her bedroom one night and asked, "Daddy, have you talked to God about my illness?" "Yes, I have," he said. "What did he say?" she asked.

When Praying Is Difficult

There are a lot of us who have to confess there are times when we pray that we do not seem to get through. We seem to get a busy signal. The circuits are jammed. We seem to be on a permanent "hold." We are unable to communicate effectively with God. Our prayers go unanswered and seem so useless and futile. I confess that I really do not understand people for whom praying is always so easy.

When you read about the great saints of Christendom, praying was often a struggle for them, too. We discover that we join hands with a host of others through the centuries who have also found that praying was not easy.

Moses had led the children of Israel through the wilderness to the edge of the Promised Land. He prayed he might be able to go into that Promised Land, but he went no further than Mount Nebo. His prayer to enter the Promised Land was not granted.

Jeremiah prophesied the destruction of Jerusalem by enemies from the North who would invade the holy city and bring great

---

2   C.S. Lewis, *A Grief Observed* (San Francisco: Harper & Row, 1989), 18.

desolation. He became a mockery and laughing stock of the city. He sat alone in isolation and prayed: "Oh, God, deliver me. Where are you?"

The psalmist lifted up his voice and cried: "Oh, God, my adversaries taunt me all the day long saying 'where now is your God?'"

The Apostle Paul wrote, "I entreated the Lord three times that my thorn in the flesh might be removed, but each time I was told God's grace was sufficient."

In the Garden of Gethsemane Jesus kneeling in great agony cried, "Oh, Father, if it is possible, let this cup pass from me." But it did not. He died in great suffering and agony upon a cross.

WHEN PRAYER DOESN'T SEEM TO WORK

Praying has not always been easy for many people. Sometimes prayer is so easy for some because they have not yet confronted any great crisis or difficulty. Others have taken various approaches to prayer. I mention only two. There are some who have had difficulty in their prayer life and declare: "I have tried prayer, and it doesn't work, so I will no longer do it." You know about these people, maybe you are one of them. They have certain things, desires, ambitions, wants or expectations, so they pray for them. Their hopes are not realized, and, therefore they say that prayer is useless. "It didn't work," they assert.

This attitude reminds me of a young woman who gets married and buys a cookbook and decides to bake a chocolate pound cake. She reads the recipe and follows it, she thinks, line-by-line, and then places the cake in the oven. Later she brings the burnt offering to her husband. It is a disaster. She looks at the result of her efforts. Its appearance is sad. She and her husband taste it and it is unbelievably bad. She throws the cookbook out the window and says, "This proves that this cookbook is no good." But we know better, do we not?

A young man has been eager to buy a computer. He selects a small one, brings it home, and finally figures out how to connect all the wires. He turns it on and gets nothing but mass confusion on the screen. He works with it for a while, reads the instructions again but nevertheless, he cannot get it to work. He calls the store where he bought it and complains, "This computer is no good. It doesn't work." The salesman asks, "Have you tried so and so?" "Oh," is the response.

There is a man who buys a book on how to play golf. He reads how he is supposed to stand, keep his head down, and how he is supposed to hold the club. He finally takes his swing and off goes a clump of grass and dirt as he misses the ball altogether. He throws his book and clubs away and declares, "They are no good at all. They did not teach me a thing." Or a young student who takes two piano lessons, and then sits down to play numbers by Bach and Beethoven and concludes: "I can't do it. My music teacher is no good." Isn't it interesting the different conclusions we sometimes reach with insufficient and inadequate information. We can quickly make a judgment about why something does or doesn't work.

SOME ASSUME THAT PRAYER IS FOR THE WEAK OR CHILDREN

We may take another approach. We assert that prayer is really for children, for the insufficient, the weak - those who are not really in control of him or herself or life. I remember visiting a man in the hospital. He was not a church member, but was the relative of one of our church members. As I got ready to leave, I asked him if he would like me to have a word of prayer with him. There was no response. I knew he was hard of hearing.

"Jake," his sister said. "He wants to know if it is okay if he has a word of prayer with you."

"I heard him," Jake responded. "I don't guess it will do any harm."

It took me a moment to compose myself to offer that prayer. There are some people for whom prayer has little meaning. They view prayer as being reserved for those who might need it. "It won't hurt anything but it sure won't do any good either," they declare.

PERSONS WHO HAVE HELPED ME IN MY UNDERSTANDING OF PRAYER

In my own struggle to find prayer meaningful, I have found that it has been a slow process. Down through the years, it has become meaningful to me because of individuals I have known for whom it was significant and through reading the writings of persons who found prayer helpful. I will never forget hearing the prayers of D. L. Lohr, a deacon in the first church I served as pastor. I felt that every time this uneducated farmer, who was very close to God, prayed, I was moved into the very presence of God. In another church, I used to visit Mrs. Mae Jobes, who was ninety-two years old, and she would always tell me about the Psalm she had memorized that week and about the people for whom she had been praying. She always asked me to pray for her, but when I left she had encouraged me by her own prayer life.

Allen Turner was a medical doctor whose practice came to an end because of rheumatoid arthritis. When I would go visit Dr. Turner, he would always tell me about the Bible study, which he had done, and what he had learned new about God in his own devotional life. I will never forget the prayers of Dr. William Mueller, a professor I had in seminary. He was a great church historian but a deeply devout man whose prayers moved his listeners into a sense of the presence of God.

HELP FROM THE WRITINGS OF OTHERS

Through the years I have read books by authors like John Baillie, a great Scottish theologian, who wrestled with hard questions of the faith and yet had a deep devotional life. There was a corner in his study where a bookcase stood that was filled with devotional books and various translations of the Bible, and a kneeling pad was on the floor where each day he knelt before God. As brilliant a theologian as he was, Baillie knew that he needed the power that came through prayer.

Persons like Harry Emerson Fosdick, Leslie Weatherhead, Elton Trueblood, George Buttrick, Elizabeth O'Connor, Joyce Rupp, John Killinger, C. S. Lewis and a host of others have enabled me to see the meaning of prayer. These persons have taught me that I could use my mind, wrestle with the deep questions of the faith, and still find the reality of the presence of God through prayer. They helped me to see that prayer was not gibberish as so many are prone to make it.

LEARNING FROM THE CRISES OF LIFE

Many of the psalmists often wrote about their personal struggles and how God responded to their prayers. The psalmist who wrote the 116th Psalm, had evidently gone through an awful crisis in his life. He had probably come close to dying. In this psalm we read how he came to the Temple to offer God a thanksgiving sacrifice. God, he notes, had heard his prayer, and he had experienced deliverance. His heart was filled with gratitude and he felt compelled to express his feelings. You and I may have sometimes sensed something of the reality of God through our own struggles with praying like the psalmist did.

Let me share with you a few things that have helped make prayer more meaningful for me. This list is obviously not complete but is only suggestive.

MY KNOWLEDGE IS LIMITED

The first thing which helped me was the awareness that my own knowledge is very limited. I sometimes do not really know what I should pray for and neither do you. What in the world would happen if God granted every prayer that was ever asked? Some prayers are selfish. Some are egotistical. Some may be totally foolish. God is an utter stranger to many people. Nevertheless, they expect God to respond immediately to whatever they want at the moment. When my children were small (and now my grand-children), they would sometimes ask if they could have ice cream or a candy bar or a soft drink a short while before they were to eat a main meal. You and I know, however, that simply because they wanted it didn't mean they should have it. My wife and I knew it would spoil their meal, so we didn't give them what they wanted.

Sometimes, to grant the form of somebody's request, many actually deny the essence of what they really need. No clearer example of this to me can be found than the prayers for the conversion of Augustine in the Middle Ages. When Augustine was a young man, he was a scholarly rebel and not a Christian. His mother was a devoted Christian and prayed that he might be converted. He told her that he planned to go to Milan. She had been praying for his conversion and was afraid that if he went there he would never be converted. So she got down on her knees and prayed that God would not let him go to Italy. But he went to Italy. While he was there he came under the influence of one of the great preachers of the time, Ambrose, and he was converted. If God had granted her second prayer, he could never have fulfilled the first. Sometimes we really do not know how we should pray. We need to make our requests known to God but remember that God knows the deeper, real need in our lives.

GOD EXPECTS US TO USE OUR OWN RESOURCES

We need to be aware that God is not going to do something for us that he expects us to do ourselves. God is not going to do something for you that you can do. He expects you to use your mind, your strength, and your own ability to accomplish whatever you can.

Several years ago two young men came into my study. They said that they were missionaries to our city. I talked with them for a while about their work. They told me that they were looking for a church with a certain kind of preacher who satisfied all of their particular prescribed approaches. In the course of the conversation,

I tried to encourage them to get some further education. They were very young men and had never been to college.

"We don't need to go get any more education," they said. "If God wants us to know something, he will give it to us."

"Oh, really? Suppose he calls you to be a missionary to France," I asked. "Will you be able to speak French?"

"Certainly," they responded. "All we have to do is pray and instantly we will know how to speak French."

"That is interesting," I said, "because there have been thousands of missionaries who have gone to countries all over the world, and I do not know a single one of them anywhere who has not had to go to language school or to spend long hours and years learning the language. What you call prayer is not prayer," I continued. "It is magic."

God is not engaged in magic. He expects you to use your mind to accomplish something. If prayer is like magic, why would you or I hire a contractor to fix our roof if it had a hole in it? Why not just gather on our front lawn and sit down and pray, "God give us a new roof," and presto there it is? Why should we be worried about any debts we have if all we have to do is pray?

Do you believe that all you have to do is to pray and ask for God's help, and God will automatically fill up your bank account with money or that God will just wipe out your debt? If that is true, why do any of us need to work? We could just go home and pray and put a basket under our bed at night and let God fill it up with money. That is not prayer. That is nonsense, foolishness, and magic. Unfortunately that seems to be some people's concept of prayer. God wants us to use our mind, heart, ability, strength, and efforts. He does not do for us what he expects us to do for ourselves.

Prayer Is Not Restricted by Time, Space or Place

I have found that prayer is not limited to a certain place or time. There obviously are times that you need to be alone to pray. You need to find your closet, quiet place, study, chair, or desk and be alone. Sometimes the most meaningful praying that you will ever do may be done in unusual places and come unexpectedly.

A noteworthy painting by Jean-François Millet shows a chapel where peasants, who have just left the field in response to the bell which called them to prayer, are seen kneeling. The mud from the fields where the men have been laboring is visible on their boots. There is something lovely about the picture, but there is also something that seems very wrong. Individuals need time for prayer in the church. But if this is the only time that you pray, you have not really begun to understand prayer.

You should be able to pray at the desk where you work, by the kitchen sink as you wash dishes, while you make the bed, while you are cutting the grass, as you drive the car, while you care for the children, or a quiet moment at your job. Prayer needs to be a vital part of all of your life. You can pray while you are shopping in a store, working in the fields, operating on a patient, speaking in a law court, teaching a class, working on a car as a mechanic, typing a letter, or with your eyes wide open as you drive your car. All the opportunities in life can become occasions for prayer and not just the isolated moments you might have for quiet, private reflection.

LIVE IN COOPERATION WITH THE NATURAL LAWS OF THE UNIVERSE

We also need to learn to understand and cooperate with the spiritual and natural laws of God. To avoid making prayer some kind of magical phenomenon, we need to understand God's laws and seek to live by them. If there were no natural laws of God, think of the chaos that would exist in the world. If you had no assurance that the chair you are sitting on would remain solid, how could you remain seated? Suppose it could change into an alligator? If the chandelier in your dining room could suddenly become a pumpkin, or your automobile could turn into a tricycle leaving nothing in life dependable, what kind of universe would it be? The world would seem to have gone mad. But God has created a world in which natural and spiritual laws do function. We have to learn to live in cooperation with them.

If I drive across one of the bridges over the Chesapeake Bay or the James River and have an accident in which my car goes off the bridge and plunges toward the water, I can and will pray. But my prayer will not be for God to bring my car back on the bridge. I do not believe that is going to happen for a moment. The law of gravity will be enforced. This does not mean that God is imprisoned within his laws. He is not. Even the miracles of Jesus, which are recorded in the New Testament, are not a violation of natural laws. They are revelations of higher laws that we may not be able to see nor understand at this particular moment.

For centuries men and women thought that iron could not float. But when it was formed into a certain shape and made into a ship, it could float. Nobody thought that iron could fly. When iron is shaped in the form of an engine, it can make an airplane lift its wings into the sky. Are there violations of natural laws here? No. There are other natural laws which are being followed.

I love the story George Truett told about a man who said that the law of gravity could never be violated. A man, who was sitting nearby whittling, heard a man make that statement and asked: "What is that you say?"

"The law of gravity can never be violated," the man said. "Whatever goes up will come down."

"Is that so?" the whittler responded. He took his pocketknife and threw it up into the ceiling and it adhered to the ceiling and did not fall back.

Is that a violation of the law of gravity? Of course not! There is another physical law in operation. When we sent the Voyager 1 far out into space, which has indeed escaped our gravity, even our solar system, and won't be back, does that mean that our gravity is no longer functioning? Of course not. There are other laws in operation. We need to learn to live and cooperate with these natural and spiritual laws as well or we will break ourselves against them.

WE DO NOT KNOW OUR OWN DEEPEST NEEDS

Finally, you and I need to be aware that we can never voice our own deepest prayer needs. The inner spirit of God will pray those for us. This is a part of what Paul was saying in the great eighth chapter of Romans. "Likewise the Spirit helps us in our weakness; for we do not know how to pray as we ought, but that very Spirit intercedes with sighs too deep for words" (8:26 NRSV). There are times when you and I attempt to pray and our prayers are really only "sighs" or "groans" – the inarticulate expressions of our innermost needs. We can't verbalize our deepest needs. But the Holy Spirit within us voices our feelings, needs, and hopes to the heart of God. Daniel Vestal acknowledges that there are times in our lives when words are inadequate to express our emotions and we can only "sigh or vent with an inarticulate utterance."[3] Our real needs and hopes, of which we ourselves may not even be aware, are expressed by God's spirit within us (Romans 8:26-27). There are several passages where groaning is mentioned in the New Testament. One of these references is found when the Pharisees asked Jesus for a sign (Mark 8:11-13). He groaned within his spirit because of their desire for a sign. Another reference is seen in the passage when Jesus is in the Garden of Gethsemane and he prayed with loud groans (Luke 22:39-44). His deepest needs were like groans voicing his agony to God.

In our times of loneliness, depression, suffering, grief, or what-ever our experience is, we might not be able to verbalize it but God senses it. He knows our need. He understands it, because the Holy Spirit makes intercession for us.

When you and I seek to pray, we should go to the master of all prayers, Jesus Christ, our Lord. We look to him for guidance in our prayer life. When the disciples sought help from him, they did not ask, "Lord teach us to preach." They did not ask, "Lord, teach us how to teach," nor "Lord, teach us how to do miracles." They

---

3   Daniel Vestal, *Being the Presence of Christ* (Nashville: Upper Room Books, 2008), 18.

requested, "Lord, teach us how to pray." They had seen something in his life about prayer which was radically transforming. At the beginning of each day, at the conclusion of each day, and before every important event in his life, they had seen Jesus pray. They asked him, "Lord, teach us how to pray." Should that not be a request for the journey of our lives? "Lord, teach me that the inner person might be strengthened, fortified, and built up and I might truly become what you would have me to be."

During the Second World War, a young soldier was petrified as he was about to leap from his plane behind enemy lines. He came over to the chaplain and asked, "Chaplain, will you pray that I will come through this jump safely and I will not be harmed?" The chaplain put his arm around the young paratrooper and said, "Son, I can't pray that prayer. But I tell you what I will do. When you jump, I will jump with you, and we will pray that we will sense the presence of God with us in the midst of whatever happens. Remember, that whether we live or die, nothing can separate us from him."

No, we really don't get a busy signal when we pray. Even when our prayers seem to go unanswered, let us wait in quiet confidence and trust that God does hear us. In our grief, despair or concern, trust God with assurance that God indeed gathers our concerns and bears them with loving grace and assurance. Though all else fail, pray with assurance that God indeed will ultimately prevail. Heaven is not made of brass. God hears us. God answers every prayer that we make. Sometimes it is "no." Sometimes it is "wait." Sometimes his answer is, "I am working out something else." Everything that happens is not necessarily God's will, but we have the assurance that God is working in all things for good to those who love him. God is present with us in the worst kinds of circumstances. God will continue to bring good to those who love him. God will sustain us and nothing can ever separate us from God's presence. Pray without ceasing.

Oh, God who speaks to us in our stillness and our silence, speak to us now silently. Oh, God who speaks to us in our noise and our rushing, speak to us in the sound of your coming. Oh, God who speaks to us in our coming and going, speak to us in the movement of your presence. Oh, God who speaks our thoughts and needs even when they are inexpressible, speak to us and through us even now. Amen

CHAPTER 2

PRAYING
WITH
UNDERSTANDING

A number of years ago an architectural firm ran an advertisement in the Chicago Sun Times stating that they would build a house with a special room eight feet by ten that could be devoted entirely to prayer. This "prayer room", they advertised, would be "a home with a religious heart." They, of course, put a footnote on their ad so that, if a person got tired of their prayer room, it could be turned into a den, card room, or sewing room, or something else.

I suppose every home really needs a religious heart. We need to have some place within our home that is devoted to prayer. It need not be a room built and designed by an architect for that purpose, but prayer needs to be a central ingredient in our lives. It is interesting to discover that studies have revealed people who do not even believe in God sometimes pray. I am not sure to whom they offer their prayer, but they still pray. In a survey of church members across our country, one of the items they listed first on which they would like to hear sermons is prayer. We all want to pray more effectively.

WHY SHOULD WE PRAY?

Prayer Is an Opening to the Mystery of the Universe

Why should we pray? I pray because it is a way of seeking to open myself to the mystery of the universe itself. I long to make an affirming connection with God. I reach beyond myself to be open to the Source of Life itself and to link myself with the Center of the universe itself – the power of God. I do this with the awareness that my strength is always inadequate and insufficient. I learned a long time ago that I have only tapped the edge of all that there is within myself and within the universe itself.

A number of years ago, when our children were small, we took them for their first trip to the beach. After playing in the sand and water a while, they came running to us with their sand pails and said: "Mother, Daddy, look, we have the ocean in our buckets!" Oh, they had a pail full of water, but they did not have the entire ocean in their buckets.

There are too many of us, especially in religious circles, who wear theological and holy caps and like to proclaim, "We have got God in our pockets!" But we have only begun to touch the edge of the garment of the universe. I spent many years in theological education and have read hundreds of books. I have learned Greek and Hebrew and other scholarly languages and have poured over theological, religious, and biblical tomes, but I want to confess to you that when it comes to understanding God I still feel like a small boy looking through the knothole in a fence. I have only begun to catch a glimpse of what God is like. How can anyone dare make the audacious claim that he or she has the ultimate handle on God? That is a blasphemous statement. We are always in pilgrimage, and we have certainly never arrived in our knowledge of God.

The universe is like a spider's web to me. No matter where you touch its edge, you feel the shivering of God's presence upon it. There is no place in the world you can go – the furthest corner of the planet, stand before a starving child, enter a home of great wealth, climb a mountain peak, or cross a desert-- and you still touch the corner of the garment of God. The mystery of his presence overshadows us everywhere. But isn't it astounding how we can be in some back inlet of the world and think that this small body of water is the universe itself? We assume that our shallow inlet contains all of God, when just a few yards beyond the breaking of the waves lies the immense ocean itself. We are only on the edge of it and have not yet launched into its depths. Too many think they can contain all of God in their small mud puddles.

I pray because I want to open myself to the mystery of the being of God. I seek to open myself to the Source of life itself – the Creator and Redeemer. Prayer is essential to life as food is to survival, as air is to breathing, as light is to seeing, as sound is to hearing. Prayer is an essential part of the vitality of our existence, and without it we do not build ourselves into the right relationship with God that awaits us.

Prayer is a means of raising one's consciousness to the sensitivity of God's presence. We seek to be drawn into God's thoughts and we try to lift our own thinking to an awareness beyond our own selfish desires and lose our thinking in an awareness of the presence of Another. Prayer is a deep seated yearning to be open to the reality that there is a Power beyond our own resources which can inform and guide us.

Pray Out of a Sense of Need

I have found that I pray most sincerely out of a deep sense of need. Who among us does not have needs which we cannot answer and so we reach up to God to hear his spirit answer? Look at the eighty-sixth Psalm for a moment. The writer of Psalm 86 had gone through a terrible experience. The word "day" in verse seven is not a reference to clock time but denotes an experience that had brought him close to the face of death itself where he experienced the judgment of God. Out of that calamity, he found deliverance, and now he voices thanksgiving to God for his grace.

The parable in Luke 18:1-8 recounts the story about a widow who was in a hopeless situation. In ancient time a widow would never go before a judge herself. This judge was obviously not a Jewish judge. In the Jewish legal system there were never less than three judges. This judge was gentile, most likely a Roman judge. Women usually did not speak in public. For this woman to plead her case as she did obviously meant that her husband was dead, or she was divorced, or had no sons. The fact that she was making her own petition before the judge indicates that she was in a hopeless position with a deep personal need. Put this parable on hold. We will come back to it in a minute for its help to us here.

Some persons may try to deny the reality of God but the roots of need are still deep within them. The roots of religion are also buried deep within us. Though we may sometimes deny God with the top of our mind, as John Baillie writes, in the bottom of our heart there is still an echo of his presence. Henry Mitchell illustrates this point in his story about some prostitutes who had become hardened to religion. These prostitutes had denied God with their words and living for a long time. One of them entered a hospital to give birth to a child with curses on her lips. But when it came time for the delivery of her baby, and as the pain increased, she reached back into the depths of her being and cried, "Oh, Lord, have mercy." We may deny God with our words but deep down within us there is still a hunger and need for his presence.

You may have heard about the young woman in Russia who was taking a civil service examination. One of the questions was, "What is the inscription on the Samaritan Wall?" She wrote down what she thought was the correct answer but wasn't sure. After the exam, she rushed over to look at the wall to see if she had put the right answer. The inscription read: Religion is the opiate of the people. "Thank God," she said, "I put the right answer."

We can deny God with the top of our mind but deep down within the recesses of our heart there is a feeling of the divine. I am aware of my own vulnerability and inadequacies. One slip in the shower, a fall off a ladder, a drunk driver crossing the road into the path of our car or a hundred other uncertainties in life demonstrates our vulnerability. I have sensed it vividly when I have stood by the graveside of a loved one. I remember those feelings of inadequacy as I stood by the hospital bedside of my wife, my children, and my parents. I remember those feelings as I lay in the hospital bed awaiting surgery myself. And who has not known feelings of hopelessness when he or she has been the victim of misunderstanding, hostility or rejection? We all know deep within us that we have unmet needs, and we cry out for the presence of God.

Guidance

I also pray out of genuine desire for guidance in my life. I know that I am inadequate to face all of the demands, concerns and decisions on my resources alone. Trying to make some of these decisions on my own is like trying to travel through a dense forest or a thick jungle or an unfamiliar city, like Washington, D.C., without a guide or a map. We need directional signs, maps and guidance to help us traverse the unknown world before us. We reach out to God's spirit to guide us along life's pathway, road or stepping-stones; otherwise we face uncertainty and confusion. Knowing my limitations and inadequacies, I reach out to live in harmony with the Creator of the universe and draw upon that divine wisdom. I want to link my life with The Eternal Source of wisdom and guidance.

Pray Out of Thanksgiving

When our deep needs have been met, this moves us to an attitude of adoration, praise, and thanksgiving. We take off our shoes because we are aware that we are on holy ground. We remove our hats, bend our knees, and lift our voices in adoration and thanksgiving to God for his abundant blessings to us. We exclaim, "Bless the Lord, oh my soul, and forget not all of his benefits." Harvey Cox wrote about a legend which depicted the angels in charge of taking prayer requests to God and those in charge of bringing thanksgivings. Those who were charged with bringing expressions of thanksgiving spent most of their time resting. But those who had to bring requests were constantly busy, because individuals were always voicing their requests to God, but they seldom expressed thanksgiving.

William Steiger, a university professor, had reached a low point in his life. Despondency, despair, and depression had overtaken his life. He was talking with a friend one day about his feelings.

"Bill," his friend advised, "why don't you try to focus on those things in your life for which you can be thankful? Learn to express appreciation for the good things you have experienced and don't focus on the bad things all the time."

"I try to do that," he said, "but it is very difficult."

"Think about somebody in your life who has really meant a lot to you," his friend urged, "and write them a thank you note. It will mean a lot to them, and it will focus your mind in a different direction."

Bill thought about his friend's advice for a while, and then he remembered a schoolteacher he had once in high school who encouraged him. So he sat down and wrote her a note. By return mail he received a letter back.

"Dear Willie," he read. "Thank you for your note. You will never know what it meant to me. I have taught school for forty-five years. I am now retired. Your letter is the first note of appreciation that I ever received. I will go to my grave thanking you for it." He was so inspired that he sat down and wrote letters to everybody that he could think of to say, "thank you."

Some Guidelines for Praying

Have you ever thought what it would do to your life if you really learned to express thanksgiving to God for all the gifts that you have? All of life is a gift, and should be celebrated. How can you accomplish what I have written about here? Let me suggest a few simple ideas.

Pray Constantly

The first thing you need to do is to be constant in your praying. Go back with me as we look again at the widow in the parable of Jesus. This was true of her, wasn't it? She was consistent and persistent. She continued to go back to the judge with her demands for justice. The words in the Greek suggest that her continual coming "would wear me out" or more literally "give me a black eye," or, translated another way, she will "give me a headache" by her continuous coming. It was not that the judge cared anything for that woman, but he just wanted to free himself from her ongoing persistence. Jesus was not saying that God is like the judge in this parable. He was using a negative illusation to encourage his disciples to follow the woman's example in being persistent when we pray.

Unfortunately we are not usually very constant in praying. For many of us, our prayers are more spontaneous, spasmodic, and occasional. There is no sense of consistency in our praying. Our prayer life is sort of like a spare tire, we use it in case of an emergency. Prayer is usually not a part of the vitality of our life. Prayer for us is often like the glass with the instructions imprinted on it: "Break in case of emergency" when you need to call the fire department. It is used only when necessary.

You may be familiar with the comic strip "Funky Winkerbean." The coach is depicted lying in bed in a hospital room. He has had an accident and his hands are folded in prayer. "God," he prays, "it's me the coach . . . I know it's been awhile since you've heard from me . . . But up till now everything's been okay!"

That's the way a lot of us pray – only in case of an emergency. Jesus calls us to consistency and perseverance in our praying. "Blessed are those who hunger and thirst after righteousness." Prayer, if it is to be meaningful, has to be a continuous habit based on determination and patience. As Jacob wrestled with the angel of God until the break of day, our prayers are not to be casual requests. We pray with the assurance that God will always respond. Repetition affirms our desire for its fulfillment. Our willingness to be persistent is a confession of how deeply our need is felt. We cry out to God that our need might be met. Our request is not casual but urgent.

Find a Place for Meditation

Second, you need to have a place of stillness and quiet. We can pray anywhere, yes, but unfortunately our awareness that we can pray anywhere often keeps us from praying somewhere in particular. Pascal, the French philosopher, once said, "The whole trouble with man is his inability to sit down in a room and be quiet." Alfred North Whitehead writes, "Religion is what the individual does with his own solitariness. It is the transition from 'God the void' to 'God the enemy', and from 'God the enemy' to 'God the companion'. Thus religion is solitariness; and if you are never solitary, you are never religious."[4] One of our cliches has been turned on its head by an old Eastern expression, "Stop doing something. Just stand there." There is the need for stillness and quiet within all of us. "Be still and know that I am God," the psalmist writes (Psalm 46:10).

Have you found a place of quietness and stillness in your home? This is a place where there is no television, radio, computer or telephone. Have you found that place of stillness in a quiet walk, some spot in your yard, a corner in the den, a chair in the living room, or kitchen? Where is that quiet spot where you open your being to God?

"Oh, I am so busy," you say. Aren't we all? But if our busyness keeps us from spending any time with God, don't blame it just on being busy. We have to blame it on the fact we really do not want to block off the time to establish that kind of relationship. Our priorities will determine whether or not we will open any avenues of quietness to God. If we are too busy, it is probably an indication that we really do not have the desire. We have to reorder our priorities.

I will write more about this later, but let me suggest that you might want to begin your meditation with a Bible reading or by using a devotional book. Begin your prayer with adoration and praise to God. Express thanksgiving for God's blessings and then confess your sins and ask for forgiveness. Next you might pray in intercession for others and then rededicate yourself to God. Conclude by being quiet and still and listening to God.

---

4   Quoted in Thomas S. Kepler, *Leaves from a Spiritual Notebook* (Nashville: Abingdon Press, 1960), 90.

The Routineness of Prayer Can Be a Deterrent

Third, do not let the familiar and routineness of prayer keep you from praying. The very fact that you and I can pray to God anytime we want, at any place, often keeps us from having a particular time and particular place for praying which prohibits our understanding of the deeper meaning of prayer. Isn't it strange that those things which are most familiar and routine to us sometimes become so much a part of our lives or our surroundings that we do not take them seriously or see their significance?

My hometown, Lynchburg, Virginia, is located less than twenty miles from Appomattox, the place where the treaty for ending the Civil War was signed. I drove past Appomattox almost weekly on my way to college. I was a college student before I stopped there and reflected on its historical significance.

My first church was thirty miles from Charlottesville, Virginia. Located on a mountain outside Charlottesville is Thomas Jefferson's prestigious home, Monticello. The first time I ever visited that historic home was when I went there with a friend who had come with me to my church. That was the first time I ever saw it, yet I had driven past it week after week for years.

My family lived in Louisville, Kentucky for fifteen years, and we discovered very quickly that many of the local residences, had not been to Locust Grove, a famous historic home in the city, which was the last home of General George Rogers Clark, the founder of Louisville. Isn't it strange that famous places which are nearby and familiar are the ones we often do not take the time to visit? The opportunity to pray anytime often becomes an excuse for not praying at certain times. Its closeness and familiarity sometimes keep us from praying often.

Every twenty-five years on Christmas Eve a door called Porta Sancta is opened in St. Peter's Cathedral in Rome. The pope leads a processional of cardinals and others up to the door. He taps on the door three times with a silver hammer, the door is opened and people pour into St. Peter's Cathedral through a passage they have never entered before. They can only go through that door once every twenty-five years.

Suppose, just suppose you could pray once every twenty-five years. Can you imagine the anticipation that would come when you knew the moment was near for you to pray? Think how you would prepare for that particular moment. Your moment to pray is coming, the hour is here. "After twenty-five years," you cry, "I can finally pray!" Because we can pray anytime, we often do not pray at all – unless it is an emergency. With that attitude, we wonder why our life does not seem to flow in the path of God, or God's presence flow into us.

Reorder Your Priorities

Next, I want to assure you that your life will be different if you pray. I know that my life is not the same when I neglect prayer. It does make a difference. Harry Emerson Fosdick wrote years ago: "Prayer is the soul of religion, and failure there is not a superficial lack for the supply of which the spiritual life leisurely can wait. Failure in prayer is the loss of religion itself in its inward and dynamic aspect of fellowship with the Eternal."[5] To be cut off from God through lack of prayer is to sever a vital relationship with him.

I have found that prayer does make my life different. I do not try to approach God and make my wishes his command. Prayer is opening my life to him so that I can be bathed in the presence of God. I seek to attune my life with his purpose. This means that sometimes my desires are not granted as I want them, but my attitude is transformed, my priorities are reordered, my life is refocused, and my relationship with others is changed.

My life is not the same whether I pray or do not pray. "He is not deaf, he listens." Karl Barth, the famous theologian wrote. "More than that he acts. He does not act in the same way whether we pray or not. Prayer exerts an influence upon God's action, even

---

5   Harry Emerson Fosdick, *The Meaning of Prayer* (New York: Association Press, 1929), 40.

upon his existence. This is what the word 'answer' means."[6] To say our prayers are answered does not mean that God always gives us what we want. To have a prayer answered is to be transformed by the presence and power of God himself.

Learn to Listen

Finally, one of the hardest things to do in praying is to stop talking and listen. We ask God so frequently for something and seldom listen to sense whether God has indeed responded to our prayers. It is hard to be still and to listen. But we need to practice this art of listening. Mother Teresa was asked once what she said to God when she prayed. "I don't talk when I pray," she responded. "I listen to God."

"What does God say?" she was asked.

"Oh, God doesn't speak. He listens," she replied.

An Example of Answered Prayer

Several years age, I read about a woman who felt she had lived a rather good life. She and her husband had been married for ten years. They loved each other and enjoyed their life together. But suddenly and unexpectedly, he came down with lung cancer. She prayed to God that he might be spared, but he died. Then she began to pray for God to fill her void of loneliness and emptiness. She took a trip from New York City, her hometown, to London. One night she walked into a small church that was lit only by some flickering candles. She was startled by some sobbing she heard. She started to leave, but noticed someone was sitting near the front of the church. She walked down to the front and found a young man sitting on the front bench pouring out his heart. She sat down by him and touched him on the shoulder and asked, "Can I help you?" He looked up at her and said, "She died. She died." He burst into tears again.

In a few moments his story began to pour out. He said he and his wife had come from Australia to London. They had lived in a

6   Karl Barth, *Prayer* (Philadelphia: The Westminster Press, 1952), 21.

poor flat. His wife gave birth to a child but shortly after the birth she died. "All the people," he said, "have been so kind – the couple who minded our baby, the strangers next door who insisted I have supper with them every night, everyone at the office – through all of them God has been answering my prayers. But I wasn't listening."

Suddenly a light seemed to turn on inside Pamela's head as she heard him say, "But I wasn't listening." The answer had come. Sure. It had come. She realized that she had not been listening very well. She began to reflect on her life and her prayers. God had not saved her husband from dying and she wondered if he answered prayers. When she prayed that God might fill her life when it was so lonely, she realized she had found support from many friends. When the first Christmas came, she was invited to their home. She had never worked outside the home before, but when she needed a job, a friend opened the way for her to find a job. She came to see that all this time she had been praying to God for an answer, but like this young man, she simply had not been listening.

On Learning to Listen

Maybe the answer that comes to us from God is never realized until we learn to listen. Prayer is not so much talking, asking, and demanding, but listening – being open to what God is seeking to give us. God always answers our prayers. He is always there. His answer may come quietly and in an unexpected way, but it will come. Attend to God's voice. Don't do all the talking when you pray. Learn to listen.

Oh, Divine Father/Mother, teach us how to pray. We know that we really do not understand those things for which we should ask and how we should respond. Teach us how to listen that we might be open and receptive to your answer. Forgive us, Lord, when we want to teach you. Teach us, Lord, how to pray. Amen

CHAPTER 3

DISCIPLINES FOR SPIRITUAL GROWTH

Speaking in the seminary chapel at Vanderbilt University several years ago, Mother Alice Kahokuoluna, from Kalaupapa Leper Colony in Hawaii, said, "I have come to the seminary to learn to pray. That is my biggest need as I face my situation." As Nels F. S. Ferre, who was a Professor of Theology at that time, heard her speak, he said that he felt very small, because he knew that he and his fellow professors could teach other things much better than they could teach people how to pray. "Before the missionaries came to Hawaii," she continued, "my people used to sit outside their temples for a long time meditating and preparing themselves before entering. Then they would virtually creep to the altar to offer their petition and afterward would again sit a long time outside, this time to 'breathe life' into their prayers. The Christians, when they came, just got up, uttered a few sentences, said Amen and were done. For that reason my people called them haolis, 'without breath' or those who fail to breathe life into their prayers."[7]

WE LIVE IN A RUSH

We are in a big rush, aren't we? We don't have much time for prayer. We are too busy with everything else. There are so many activities and demands upon us. Our job requires so much time. Our family needs attention. There is always so much to do and no real time for prayer, is there? Yet, isn't it strange, when we refuse to control those things around us, we soon discover that we are

---

7   Nels F.S. Ferré, *Strengthening the Spiritual Life* (New York: Harper & Brothers, 1951), 13.

controlled by them. Habits which are not given much attention soon dominate and control us.

THE NEED FOR DISCIPLINE

Absolute freedom is a myth. Many persons struggle with un-controllable lust, alcohol, drugs, fears, and selfishness. Soon these habits dominate our lives. Many live with the illusion that an un-disciplined, uncontrolled life means real freedom. But they have found they are in bondage to drugs, alcohol, or something else. Soon, uncontrollable habits of lust, temper, prejudice, or the quest for prestige, power, and wealth dominate our lives.

Discipline is not a welcomed word today, but discipline is essential. No one can become a great musician or even a good musician without discipline. Nobody becomes an effective ath-lete, writer or artist without discipline. Almost everything in life requires some kind of discipline if one is to reach certain goals. Isn't it strange that we expect to grow in a life of prayer and spiritual de-votion without effort? Our prayer life does not grow overnight like Jack's beanstalk. Discipline is required to develop a spiritual life.

I began practicing meditation when I was in high school after I became a Christian. It has been a lifetime challenge to try to grow spiritually. I know that I am always striving to deepen my devotional life. I am keenly conscious that I have not arrived. I, indeed everyone, is always in process. We never arrive. We are ever reaching and striving to be closer to God. There are some things that I have found helpful in my own spiritual growth, and maybe they could provide some assistance to you. I would like to suggest some brief rules or guidelines for your consideration in developing or enriching your own spiritual life.

DISCIPLINES FOR DEVELOPING THE INNER LIFE

1. A Time of Silence

Practice a time of silence. We all need to cultivate "the harvest of the quiet eye." The time you spend in aloneness and quiet will open your being so you can sense God speaking to your innermost needs. Too often we have severed our roots from God, and then we wonder why we feel pulled in so many directions. Our life is not together; we have become disconnected. We have been severed from our source. Silence enables us to reconnect our being with God. Eastern religions discovered the necessity for silence centuries ago. Silence has a central place in Hindu and Buddhist religions. Some Americans have rediscovered it through Zen Buddhism or Yoga. I heard recently that the Dalai Lama spends four hours a day in mediation. If someone from another religious tradition devotes this amount of time to his own spiritual life, how can we as Christians not strive to improve our own? Several years ago I took a short spiritual retreat at the Abbey of Gethsemani in Kentucky. I was profoundly affected by the dedication of the monks to their vows of silence and prayer. The impact of that experience still remains with me and continues to challenge my spiritual life.

The Christian tradition of silence reaches back to the ancient Hebrew people where Abraham and Moses experienced God in their times of solitude. An examination of the life of Jesus, the master teacher, reveals that he often sought time of solitude. Before every major decision and significant event in his life, Jesus went apart from his disciples to be alone and pray. After he was baptized by John, he spent forty days in silence and fasting. He went apart to pray before he selected his disciples, and before the transfiguration. After the Last Supper and before his arrest, he prayed in Gethsemane at night while his disciples slept. And he prayed on the cross as he was dying. He often went apart to pray at night or early in the morning. He knew the necessity for those times of silence.

Yet many of us spend little time in silence. We are surrounded by noise at work, the TV and radio blare at us at home, and the roar of traffic pounds in our ears as we drive. Shoppers buzz around us in the stores, cell phones are constantly chirping, and many have a listening device plugged into their ears or have their eyes glued to their computer, laptop or BlackBerry. Voices cry all around us for time and attention. It's hard to find silence.

On one occasion the deacons in one of my former churches went on a weekend retreat. One of the items built into the program was thirty minutes of silence. On Saturday morning, following breakfast, each deacon was given the opportunity to spend some time in quiet meditation. During this time they were encouraged not to speak to one another. Each one could use the time as he or she wanted to. They walked, prayed, sat down and read the Scriptures, and reflected in thirty minutes of quiet. This time of silence gave them an occasion to attach themselves once again to God. When the evaluations for the deacon retreat were collected, this time of silence was selected by most of the group as the most meaningful part of the retreat. One of the deacons observed it was the first time he could remember when he had a few moments of uninterrupted, quiet time.

We need to structure a time of silence in our lives. Let me suggest two books that can help you accomplish that goal. Nurturing Silence in a Noisy Heart by Wayne Oates offers instruction on how to try to cultivate silence in your spiritual life. Morton Kelsey's book, The Other Side of Silence: A Guide to Christian Meditation, offers valuable instruction on developing the inner life. Find a time for silence.

2. Find a Place for Meditation

You have got to have a place for meditation. This place needs to be located where you are not disturbed by television, radio, computer, BlackBerry or the telephone. Take the telephone off the hook; turn off the TV, radio, cell phone and other "gadgets." Locate a quiet place. Where is that place for you? You must discover it for yourself. It may be in your easy chair, on your patio or in a park nearby. It may be in your bedroom where you can kneel by your bed. Your quiet place may be at your breakfast table when the rest of the family has gone or at your office desk when no one else is around.

I spent several summers working in a Boy Scout camp in the Blue Ridge Mountains of Virginia. One of the nice things about wilderness living was that everyone went to bed really early. I always got up at least an hour before the others began to stir so I could go down by the lake and be alone for a while. In that hour, I opened myself to the presence of God. Surrounded by mountains and the quiet sounds of the water, I read the Scriptures and "listened" in silence to God. To this day, I find myself returning in my mind's eye to those mountains again and again for spiritual nourishment. I long for that kind of quiet, uninterrupted place again.

You also need to find some small, quiet moments in your life. If you live in a busy city, you may want to eat lunch away from everybody to snatch a few minutes of peace. Take a bag lunch to work or buy something and go sit in a park by yourself for a few moments, and let your inner life come together again. You may find quiet in a brief walk or in a park near where you work or live. Find an appropriate place where you can be silent. You have to discover the place for yourself where you can "be still" and listen for God's quiet presence.

3. Find the Time

You have got to have a particular time to meditate. You need to set a time for quiet. We usually find time to eat. You may miss a meal occasionally, but you will find some time to catch up when you miss a meal. We make time for our jobs, families, sleep, and other things, but isn't it interesting we never seem to be able to find the time for silence and spiritual meditation? We will never find the time; we have to set the time. Put it on your calendar. Make a time.

What time is best for you? I don't know. You must experiment to see what the best time is for you. Find it and then keep the same time each day. For some, early morning is not their time. Bill Adler notes this point in his book, *Dear Pastor.* "Dear Pastor," a young girl writes, "We say grace at our house before every meal except at breakfast. Nobody talks at breakfast. Yours truly, Sally, age 11."[8] It is hard to meditate if you are not awake.

Don't try to select a time when you are already exhausted. Your time of meditation cannot be too helpful if you are so tired you can hardly stay awake, much less think and be open to God. This means a few minutes before you go to bed may not be the best time for you. Remember to be faithful in your use of this time. Having set a particular hour, stick with it. It is probably wise to begin your time of meditation as a brief period. Don't say, "Well, I'll start with an hour." If you are not accustomed to meditation, you may find an hour an unbelievably long period of time. I would suggest you begin with a few minutes and gradually increase the time a little bit each day. Start with a brief period of meditation and add more time as you find it more meaningful.

4. Learn to Relax

Learn to relax when you come to your time of meditation. All of the great mystics through the ages have written about the importance of learning how to breathe properly to help in relaxation. Inhale and take in a deep breath, then exhale. Repeat for a few moments to relax your body. Try also to relax your mind. Breathing slowly and "doing nothing" is a way of trying to focus your mind, bodily senses, emotions and total being to an "awareness" of the Breath of God which is within and around, his all-consuming Presence. Let your whole being slow down so God can speak to you. Slowly turn your thoughts away from your busy life to discovering the peace of God. You are giving the attentiveness of the moment to the intention of opening yourself to the deep mystery of the Presence of God. Use some breathing exercises to help you relax and move into that state. Open yourself completely to God.

---

8   Bill Adler, *Dear Pastor* (Nashville: Thomas Nelson, 1980).

5. The Position of Prayer

Find whatever form or posture is helpful for you as you pray. You do not always have to kneel to pray. There were occasions when Jesus knelt but, at other times, he stood or sat to pray. There are many positions you can use to pray. In college I often knelt beside my bed at night when I prayed. Sometimes I would be so tired I would fall asleep kneeling by the bed. I have often wondered how effective my prayers were when I was so exhausted and tired at the end of the day that I would fall asleep. I obviously needed a better time to pray when I could be more alert and able to pray.

Through the years I have learned that I can pray sitting at my desk, when I'm lying down or standing, walking, sometimes even when I'm jogging, or sometimes while I'm driving the automobile-- with my eyes wide open, of course. We can pray in many different positions and in many places. You determine the posture that is most helpful and meaningful to you. You may have to experiment to discover what is most helpful for you. Particular needs may determine different positions. Deep repentance may force you to your knees. A sense of shame or guilt may make you unable to lift your eyes toward heaven. Grief may awaken you in the night as you lie in bed. I find I pray best most of the time while I sit at my desk with my Bible and other devotional helps before me as I open myself to God.

6. Resources for Meditation

Learn to use other resources to help you pray and meditate more effectively. I have drawn on many helps through the years in my own devotional life. I have found that my own strength and knowledge are inadequate.

Magazines

Some of you might find magazines like *The Upper Room, Reflections Devotional Guide, Weavings, Alive Now, Our Daily Bread,*

Micah Challenge, or *Guideposts* helpful. These offer daily or occasional guidance.

Books

Some books that have aided me in developing the inner life are *The Imitation of Christ* by Thomas á Kempis, *A Serious Call to A Devout and Holy Life* by William Law, *New Testament of Devotion* by Thomas Kelly, *Beginning from Within* by Douglas Steere, *Search for Silence* by Elizabeth O'Conner, *The Practice of the Presence of God* by Brother Lawrence, *The Life of the Soul* by Samuel Miller, *Strengthening the Spiritual Life* by Nels F. S. Ferré, and Richard J. Foster's *Celebration of Disciplines.* Some of these books may no longer be in print but they can be acquired online from used book dealers at reasonable prices. Religious bookstores also contain many other sources for devotional help. These books are simply some resources that have been extremely helpful to me.

Persons

There are literally dozens of books that provide help for the spiritual life. Read some of them to help you on your journey of faith. These guides will take only a few minutes each day but can turn your mind to thoughts about God. Persons like John Baillie, Nels F.S. Ferré, George Buttrick, Harry Emerson Fosdick, J. B. Phillips, C. S. Lewis, Leslie Weatherhead, Harold Kohn, Frederick Buechner, Elton Trueblood, John Killinger, Joyce Rupp, Barbara Brown Taylor, John Claypool and a host of others have helped me cultivate a time of prayer in my own life.

Secular Sources

Sometimes I have drawn on individuals whose writings would be considered secular to help me in my devotional life. This may sound strange to some, but, nevertheless, these persons have been inspiring to me. Archibald Rutledge, Dag Hammerskjold, Loren Eiseley, Alan Patan, and many others have fed my own spirit. You can also meditate through looking at art, listening to music, reading poetry or contemporary literature, especially selected fiction writers. The resources are endless. Whatever opens a pathway for you to commune with God is fine. Experiment and discover what resources are most useful to you. What aids one person will not necessarily be effective for someone else.

The Computer

There are many resources on the computer to provide you guidance in your meditation, both from Christian and other world religions. Among dozens of web links or sites available, I have found these helpful: Beliefnet.com, Prayer of the Day, explorefaith.org or you can just Google "prayer and meditation." Some people are more comfortable using resources from the computer than others. But for those who are comfortable with this tool, these websites can provide many helpful suggestions and guidelines.

Books of Prayers

You may also find books of prayers very helpful. John Baillie's *A Diary of Private Prayer* is one of my favorites. Harry Emerson Fosdick's *A Book of Public Prayers*, Robert Raines' Lord, *Could You Make It A Little Better?*, *The Prayers of Peter Marshall*, Walter Rauschenbusch's *Prayers of the Social Awakening*, William Barclay's *The Plain Man's Book of Prayers*, Michel Quoist's *Prayers*, and many others have compelled me to grow in my prayer life. Reading the prayers of others can feed your own life as you are nurtured by them.

The Bible

Our chief resource is, of course, the Bible. Like the ancient psalmists, we delight in the "law of God." The word which the psalmist used to depict meditation is the same word which is used to describe "a cow chewing its cud" or "the murmuring of a dove." The point is that the reader is thoroughly absorbed in the Scriptures. As you muse over the Scripture, immerse yourself in their meaning until they become a part of your very being. Let your roots draw deeply from the refreshing water of the Word which provides a limitless resource for spiritual growth.

Hymns

Hymns and contemporary praise and worship songs also provide an excellent source for devotional reading. Next to the Bible, our hymnal probably has influenced our thinking more than any other book. Select a hymn like "Joyful, Joyful, We Adore Thee," or "God of Grace and God of Glory" and reflect silently on the words. Select a hymn which fits your need and meditate on the words. You might also sing or chant them softly to express your own feelings of praise, sinfulness, and grace. I have found that reflecting privately on the words of a hymn often sets the tone for further meditation or gives me a song to carry with me in my heart.

A Prayer Journal

I would also encourage you to keep a prayer journal. Have you ever kept a diary? A prayer journal is similar in some ways. In this journal you record your own spiritual and devotional development. You might write down a note about the person or persons for whom you are praying today. You note in your journal something about the individual who has a special burden. As you pray for your wife, or husband, children or parents, or friends who have special problems, you note it in your journal. You pray in intercession for them. You may list your own particular needs in that moment as you pray before God. This journal is a way of examining your own spiritual growth. It becomes a mirror of your inner life. These notes are not for others to see, but only for your eyes.

A few pages from mine reveal statements like: "Lord, it is really hard for me to pray today. I didn't feel just right. I had feelings that did not make me want to come to this moment." On another occasion, "Lord, they are coming now. They need some help, and I don't know what to tell them. Their life is in a mess. What do I say?" On another occasion, "Lord, I felt you very close to me today. Your presence was real and strong. Thank you." In your own prayer journal you can record your struggles, agonies, joys, sorrows, hopes, dreams, needs, and something about your pilgrimage toward becoming more like God.

7. Practice Confession

Practice confessing during your prayer time. Our prayers have to begin with "Lord, be merciful to me a sinner." Even if you are a Christian, you are still a sinner, and this awareness directs you to begin with a prayer of confession. There are times that my sense of sinfulness is overwhelming, and I am astounded at others who do not seem to sense their own sinfulness. I am deeply aware of the neglect of my family, things that I should do, persons I have hurt with words said too quickly or deeds not done, ways that I have misunderstood others, or reacted to something that they may have said. I have a sense of guilt, and I pray for forgiveness. I know that I am unworthy of God's great love and I fall prostrate before God asking for his forgiveness and mercy.

There was a young father who had an angry conversation with his wife. He stormed out the front door, slamming it behind him, and got into his automobile. He quickly backed down the driveway, felt a bump, and knew instantly what he had done. His two-year-old child had been playing in the driveway and he had killed him in a moment. He found that he could not live with what he had done. Day after day he agonized with his guilt. He went to a psychiatrist and talked out his feelings. He became devoutly religious. He went to church on every occasion, and still he could not overcome his horrible feeling of guilt.

Finally in a church service one day, when the minister was talking about the words of Jesus on the cross, he heard the words Jesus prayed, "Father, forgive them for they know not what they do." Suddenly a light went on inside his head. He realized that if God could forgive men and women for what they had done to his Son, this same God could forgive him for what he had done to his own son.

Confession plays a significant part in a meaningful prayer life. As sinners, we hunger to experience the grace and forgiving love of God.

8. Obedience to God

Another dimension in our praying is obedience. Having experienced God's grace, we have to be obedient to his will and set our lives to be attuned with him. If we are to be his children, we have to be obedient. Many of us have gone only halfway with Christ, but the most difficult part is going the other half and committing our lives fully to him. We want to bargain with God too much, don't we? We are like the small child who wrote in Children's Letters to God, "Dear God, I wrote you before, do you remember? Well, I did what I promised. But you did not send me the horse yet. What about it? Signed Lewis."[9]

When I was in college, I wanted to go as a summer missionary to Hawaii. I prayed to God that I might be selected. I told God that if I were selected I would become a missionary. I was selected and spent the summer in mission work in Hawaii. I discovered in the midst of the summer's work, however, that God doesn't like for us to bargain with him. He didn't allow me to go just because I had said, "If you will do this for me, I will do something for you." While I was mediating I sensed God saying something like this to me: "Bill Tuck, you are very foolish. I don't make bargains with people. That's not why you are here this summer. Open yourself to learn from me." I discovered during my summer as a "missionary" that obedience to God was far more important than trying to bargain with God. I learned God does guide us in God's way. I came to realize the most important thing is not just what I wanted for my life but what God wills and purposes for it. My prayer is "not my will but God's be done." Inner peace comes to us when we have truly sought the mind of Christ.

---

9   Eric Marshall and Stuart Hample (compl.) *Children's Letters to God* (New York: Essandess, Special Edition, 1966).

9. Thanksgiving

Meaningful praying begins in the ability to express thanksgiving to God. Through our prayers, we express our appreciation to God for his great blessings. With the psalmist we exclaim: "Bless the Lord, O my soul, and forget not all his benefits." Think how dependent we are on God. Make a list of all the things for which you really have to be thankful. Almost everything we have in life has come to us as a gift – the air, the sun, the stars, the moon, food, and grass – all of creation is a gift. Your life itself is a gift from God. You had nothing to do with your being here and neither did I. We are a gift. Let us always express thanksgiving for these gifts. Jesus once healed ten lepers. All received cleansing, but only one came back and expressed thanks to him. We receive so much and seldom do we express thanksgiving. Our prayers ought to be filled with thankfulness. This might be the occasion to sing or chant your prayer to God through the use of a familiar hymn like "Now Thank We All Our God" or "Come Ye Thankful People" or "Let All Things Now Living" or one of your own construction from Scripture or poetry. You might chant Psalm 100, some of Jesus' words from the Sermon on the Mount like the Beatitudes or the Golden Rule or phrases from Paul like "In everything make your requests known to God in prayer and petition with thanksgiving. Then the peace of God, which is beyond our utmost understanding, will guard over your hearts and your thoughts, in Christ Jesus," (Philippians 4: 6-7, New English Bible) or Romans 8: 35-39, or I Corinthians 13.

10. Meditative Images

Let me suggest a final thought for you as you develop your inner life. I encourage you to work on some meditative images. Do several things when you try to meditate and pray. Listen. If you are inside, listen to the sounds that are in your house. You will sometimes hear the cracking and settling of the house itself. You may hear the sounds of a clock ticking, cars passing outside, rain on the roof or windowpane, but just attune yourself to listen for the "sounds of silence." If you are outside, you may listen to songs of birds; hear the sounds of car horns, the laughter of children playing or construction noises. If you are in a park and there is a creek, you hear the movement of the stream. The sounds around you may be a means of communication. Let them speak to you a message about life. Concentrate.

A friend of mine said that he was in a conversation once with Gordon Cosby in a hallway with people passing by constantly. Many of them wanted to speak to Dr. Cosby. But while Dr. Cosby was talking to my friend, he was concentrating on nobody but him. My friend said that he was amazed at his powers of concentration. Listen with the awareness that God is hearing you as though there were no others. Listen for his voice.

Observe

Observe everything that is around you. If there are birds flying, leaves waving in the breeze, insects singing, clouds floating by, rain or snow falling or whatever, attune yourself to what lies all around you. Maybe God will speak through some of the objects surrounding you and remind you that God is aware of a sparrow's flight or descent to the earth and that God knows the number of the hairs on our head, and, hopefully, this awareness will cause us to reflect on the "nearness" of God and God's concern for us. And God's presence will be more real to you.

Smell

You may sense God's presence through the aroma of bread baking, freshly brewed coffee, the perfumed scent of freshly shampooed hair, the scent of your dog nearby, the fragrance of flowers, the odor of honeysuckle, the smell of freshly mowed grass, or a hundred other ways. Allow these aromas to remind you of the cleansing, refining, healing, rejuvenating power of God.

Imagine

Open your heart to God like the earth opens itself to receive the rain which falls upon it. Picture yourself as dry soil waiting for the presence of God to nourish you. See yourself as blackened earth with snow falling upon you, covering you several inches deep with its whiteness. Let the symbolism of the white snow be a message of God's transforming grace which makes you whiter than snow.

If you are sitting by a mountain stream, or a creek, or a river, let the movement of the water symbolize the cleansing of God's spirit as he comes into your life to wash you clean from your sins and make you whole. Open your life to God like a flower responds to the sunlight, so you might be bathed in the power and presence of God's radiance. See yourself as a sandy beach where God's spirit breaks like the waves upon your life, cleansing and refreshing you.

In your mind's eye picture the nail prints in the hands and feet of Christ. Let his living spirit communicate with you. Let the symbols of bread and wine remind you of the broken body of Christ. Envision his shed blood on the cross which communicates God's grace and power to you. As you come before God in quiet meditation, remember that you cannot draw from the deep well of God's spirit by your own efforts. Christ himself is the bucket that reaches down into the reservoir of God's limitless being and brings us water to satisfy our thirst. God's grace is an ever-flowing stream from which you and I can draw the water of life. As we sink the roots of our being deeply into his soil, we are nourished and sustained. The last thing I do at night as I lie in bed is to open myself to God and pray for myself and my family. With that sense of presence and peace, I seek to rest my spirit in God's arms. You may want to google "Prayer and Meditation" on your computer and click on "audiovisuals" and find some other suggestions that might guide you further in this journey.

A small boy wrote in *More Children's Letters to God*, "Dear God, Sometimes I think I can see you. I think I saw you last night.

Is that a bad thing to say? I would like to very much. My mommy says you are always near us. Signed, Your friend, Herbert."[10]

O, God, I would like to see you everywhere. As Jacob declared "Surely the Lord was in this place and I knew it not." By the River Jabot, Jacob wrestled with God in a terrible struggle to determine his direction in life. Out of that experience he was forever changed. He was transformed from the scheming Jacob to Israel, the founder of a new nation. He arose from his night of prayer crippled from his extended struggles but with a new sense of God.

God's response to our prayer may be radically different from our expectations or desires. But God is present to us. It is we who are often not open and present to God. Let us open ourselves to God so we might experience the presence of God who is always seeking to make his divine presence known to us. A quiet time of meditation can allow God the right opportunity to meet us.

Many of us go through life surrounded by the fog of difficulties that confront us and problems that overwhelm us. We need to lock our lives onto the beam of God's spirit so he can bring us safely through all our storms and troubles. Practice the disciplines essential for spiritual growth. Don't expect to be very tall spiritually if you never work on your inner life. It requires effort. Practice the discipline of meditation. Thomas Merton has called contemplation "spiritual wonder." "Contemplation is the highest expression of man's intellectual and spiritual life," Merton observes. "It is that life itself, fully awake, fully alive, fully aware that it is alive.[11] Open yourself to God through prayer and meditation. The wonder of growing more in God's likeness lies before us and within us. Let us continue the journey.

O Loving God, we thank you for your availability to us. May we be available to you. Thank you, Divine Creator, for your openness to us.

———————

10 Eric Marshall and Stuart Hample (compl.) *More Children's Letters to God* (New York: Essandess, Special Edition, 1967).

11 Thomas Merton, *New Seeds of Contemplation* (New York: New Directions Books, 1972), 1.

May we be open to you. Teach us, Lord, how to pray. Through Christ our Lord, who is the master of prayer, we pray. Amen.

CHAPTER 4

HOW TO READ THE BIBLE TODAY

A Roman legend records that Sibyl of Cumae offered to sell the King of Tarquin nine volumes in which she had gathered all the wisdom of the world. The king felt that her price was too high and refused to buy them. She burned three of the volumes and offered to sell the six for the same price she had asked originally for nine. He still said no. She burned three more, and offered him the remaining three again at the same price she had asked originally. This time, fearful that all the volumes containing the wisdom would be lost, he purchased the remaining volumes.

A NEGLECTED BOOK

In some ways this story is a reminder of how we often approach the Bible. The wisdom of the ages is found within its covers. We discover words that describe the relationship between God and men and women, how to relate to one another, and how God has loved and redeemed us. But in our youth we do not take time to read these words and their wisdom is lost to us. In our middle age and sometimes even in old age, the offer to read the wisdom is unheeded. We have lost our opportunity again. The price is still the same. It requires, at any age, time, attention, study, and reading.

Why is it that we often do not read the Bible which is supposed to be the Church's chief source for spiritual guidance? There is no question today that the Bible is indeed a neglected book. Few actually read it and most people today are ignorant of its basic stories and teachings. Yet, almost all homes in America seem to have Bibles today. The Bible is still a national best seller. But for what purpose is the Bible used by these people who purchase it? Well, it is often filled with clippings, roses are pressed in it, pictures of children, grandchildren or relatives are often placed there for safekeeping. It may remain on a shelf in our bookcase or lie on a table somewhere in our house. It almost never gets read, except on rare, special occasions. It is a neglected book.

Some say, "The Bible is so dull! It is even dull in its appearance with its dark black or blue cover, its narrow parallel columns and small print." "I've tried to read it," some say, "but can't understand it." Others say, "I don't see what it has to do with my life today. It was written thousands of years ago and has nothing to do with our modern world." And so, unused, it collects dust.

Some airplane passengers have learned they can avoid conversation with others on the plane by carrying a Bible with them and display it at an appropriate time. One such person is a traveling salesman, I heard about, who simply gets on an airplane and reclines his seat, opens a Bible and puts it on his lap. He says nobody ever bothers him. He has found people quickly lost interest in talking with him, if he flexed a Bible.

AN UNFAMILIAR BOOK

Many people are honest to admit the Bible is really unfamiliar to them. Years ago Bruce Barton described the Bible as the "The Book nobody knows." Most people are honestly not familiar with the contents of the Scriptures. Many feel the Bible is filled with strange books. They say there are stories in the book of Revelation about a scarlet woman, a great beast, and all of those crazy numbers and names that people have tried to understand for centuries. Who knows what they really mean? The Old Testament is filled with discussions about ancient tribal rights and sacrificial systems, a prophet cursing children for calling him bald headed, thousands being slaughtered in God's name, a brother killing his own brother, rapes, incest and murder. What are we to make of all that? Who in the world can read with much satisfaction through the "begets" and all the genealogies? Can a person really enjoy reading about "who begat whom?" That's not fantastic devotional reading. But, in a few places, the begat list goes on page after page. As Karl Barth says, "There is a strange new world within the Bible," and we might add, many never discover it or do not want to.

The only place many people ever hear Scripture read at all is in a Sunday morning worship service. When the Scripture is read in some Protestant traditions, the minister may say, "This is the word of God." In some congregations they respond, "Thanks be to God." Many today, however, are not really too thankful for the Scriptures, are they? If we were, we would spend more time reading and studying them. In spite of that fact, the Bible continues to be the Church's chief authoritative source, as it has been down through its history. The Bible is authoritative to us because it has guided us into our understanding of God, God's redemption, grace, and how we are to relate to other persons. It is our primary source for understanding Christ, his Church, the history of Israel, and our Christian doctrines.

CONFUSING VIEWS OF THE BIBLE

Among the reasons some people have neglected to read the Bible are the strange interpretations they have heard which have been given to the Bible. These interpretations have led many believers down some strange side streets which are not essential for understanding the truth or genuine significance of the Bible. Yet some proponents of these beliefs have declared they are necessary if one is to understand the truth of the Bible. I believe they actually may do much more harm than good, and are really not essential to understand the truth or inspiration of the Bible. Let me mention a few of these beliefs.

Inerrancy

Some people have found the battle about the various ways to understand the Bible, and especially the inerrancy concept of the

Bible, confusing and often depicting ministerial arrogance. Unfortunately, there are some who have equated biblical authority with inerrancy and infallibility. Inerrancy and infallibility, however, are non-biblical words. They are not found within the Scriptures. These are only interpretations of Scripture. They are someone's theological concepts which are brought from outside the Bible and pressed upon the Scriptures as one way to understand them.

Isn't it strange that the reformation, under the guidance of Luther and Calvin, moved Christian believers away from an infallible church, and yet today we have some who are trying to establish an infallible book as the Church's authoritative source? If we mean by infallible as it was meant originally, "that which cannot fall or fail," then the Scriptures are infallible. Biblical scholars have found one hundred fifty thousand variations in ancient biblical texts. But in no way do these variations in the Bible fail in revealing God's love and redemption or in any other area that affects our essential understanding of God, Christ or Christian doctrine.

If anyone tries to assert that the Scriptures are inerrant in science, medicine, or history, he or she does not understand the nature or composition of the Bible. The Scriptures are pre-scientific. In the Old Testament there are references to a flat earth supported on pillars with a dome covering it. This is a pre-scientific description of our world. Does this mean we must believe the earth has four corners? Do we take the Bible literally and believe in a flat earth? Of course not. The Bible is pre-science. Does this mean our Bible today is not dependable? Of course not. We have to remember the persons who wrote the Scriptures were ordinary men who did not lose their humanity when they were inspired by God. They were not robots but real human persons and subject to human error. They were writing with their present knowledge of science or their unawareness of it, and their perspective of the world, as they understood it in their own ancient times. Marcus Borg has stated that as we enter the twenty-first century the older lenses of literalism and infallibility need to be replaced with new lenses, as the old have become for most people incredible and irrelevant. He argues for a new reading which "is about a deepening relationship with the God to whom the Bible points, lived within the Christian tradition as a sacrament of the sacred."[12]

Each Bible writer reflected on what he had seen or heard. It is not essential that the words of the Bible be inerrant to be meaningful. It doesn't change the revelation of God's message of redemptive love and grace one iota. That is constant. We should not try to press some unnecessary image, like inerrancy, on the Bible to read it and find guidance in its message.

Literalism and the Bible

The entire Bible was not written to be taken literally. Jesus is not literally a door or a shepherd. In the twenty-third Psalm the writer states, "The Lord is my shepherd." Surely this does not imply God is literally a shepherd but is a metaphor to depict God's protection, guidance, tender care and personal assurance. When the writer of Genesis Chaper 3 notes, "God 'walks' in the cool of the garden," this is surely a reference not to God actually "walking" but denotes the presence and companionship of God. The references by psalmists to trees "clapping" and mountains "dancing" are not literally true. These are figures of speech or metaphors as any reasonable person can see. To take the entire Bible literally in all places is not to take it seriously. The Bible contains parables, fables, stories, myths, poetry, proverbs drama allegories, letters, history, biography and many other kinds of literature. In the Genesis creation stories, for example, one should not read into this account our twenty-four hours for a "day," since the sun wasn't created until the third day. Determining what kind of literature we are reading in the Bible can help us interpret it more intelligently and realistically.

Some of the biblical passages are obviously historical and should be understood literally. Other passages are meant to be understood metaphorically or pictorially. The reader needs to try to ascertain, to the best of one's ability, the context of the passage

---

12 Marcus J. Borg, *Reading the Bible Again for the First Time* (New York: Harper Collins, 2001), 18.

and the right way to interpret it. This is not always easy. Most of the time common sense can help us to see the proper approach; while, on other occasions, we may need to draw upon the wisdom of biblical scholars as we study commentaries and Bible dictionaries.

Allegory

Some people have made the Scriptures a vast allegory. They have turned the Song of Songs, which is a majestic love poem of a man for his wife, into a story about Christ and his Church. This was not the original writer's intent. Others have dipped down into the Book of Daniel and Revelation and have found in these books a picture of every contemporary international villain they could possibly discover, or assurances to them that they knew exactly when Jesus would return or the Rapture would leave behind those who did not believe as they did. Rather than trying to see what the original writer was trying to describe for his day, they have fantasized images for our day.

Even writers like Augustine turned the parable of the Good Samaritan into an allegory. A hidden meaning was read into every detail. "A certain man" was Adam. Jerusalem was the heavenly city. The robbers were the devil and his angels. The Samaritan was Jesus and the inn was the Church. The innkeeper was the Apostle Paul and so forth. Rather than being a parable about relating to others in Christian love, this story became an allegory about the Christian doctrine of salvation. We need to be careful not to read into a passage whatever we want to find there. We should strive to determine what the original writer was trying to say and seek to understand that message.

The Inspired Word

Paul writes in Timothy that "all Scripture is given by inspiration"(2Timothy 3:16). It is "God breathed." Technically Paul is writing about the Old Testament. When Paul wrote his letter to Timothy, he wasn't talking about his letters. The gospels had not been written. He was referring to the Old Testament writings. After the Church gathered together the writings which are now designated as the New Testament, these writings were also understood to bear the same kind of inspiration as the Old Testament. Paul never dreamed his letters would be put together as part of a book called the New Testament. When Paul wrote "the Word of God is not bound" (2 Timothy 2:9), he was not writing about the Bible. He was writing about the "Word of Jesus Christ"– the living Word of God. This "Word" can never be bound. The "Word" which Isaiah proclaimed in 55:10-11 is the "Word" that has continued through the decades as God has bombarded the hearts of men and women to inform them of the divine will and way. "My word," Isaiah declared, "shall not return unto me void, but it shall accomplish that which I please, and it shall prosper in the thing whereto I send it" (Isaiah 55:11). Moffat translates this phrase, "It carries out my purpose." God's Word is actively bringing about God's will in the lives of men and women.

Christ Is Lord of the Scriptures

We also cannot put all Scripture on the same level. We do not have a flat Bible where every passage is on the same level with another. The Bible is not an ancient collection of proof text where one can dip down in any place she or he likes. Psalm 137:9 which reads, "Happy is the man who shall seize your children and dash them against the rock" is not on the same level with the words of Jesus, "Love your enemies." All Scripture is judged by the highest revelation we have – Jesus Christ. He is the final test. The Living Word judges the written word. The Bible is, to use Luther's phrase, "The Manger of Christ."

The Church's Source of Authority

In spite of the nonsensical things some have written and said about the Bible, it continues to remain the chief source of authority for the Church. Through it God continues to speak the divine message of love, grace, and redemption to us. The Bible enriches our life because it came to birth out of the lives of people. Its primary concern is not with abstract speculation or obscure thinking but with life itself. There are sixty-six different books in the Bible – thirty-nine in the Old Testament and twenty-seven in the New Testament.

The oldest book was written probably around 1300 B.C. The other books were written over a period of about fifteen hundred years. The books in the Bible were written and collected over a long period of time. They did not fall out of the sky one day or suddenly appear.

The Bible records the story of the struggle of men and women to find meaning and purpose in their lives. It traces the story of the nation of Israel and its struggle to become free from bondage, its birth as a nation, their difficulties in being God's people, their defeats and victories, their sins and accomplishments, their frustrations and needs. The New Testament contains the gospels about Jesus Christ, the history of the young church, Paul's epistles and other pastoral letters and the Apocalypse from the Isle of Patmos.

THE BIBLE IS ALIVE WITH MEANING

The Bible is a book about real life. It depicts Abraham's strength and weakness; reveals Jacobs' tragedy, his scheming as well as his fidelity, Moses' anger and assurance, David's courage, faith and sinfulness, Job's pain and suffering, Jeremiah's prophecy and lament, Elijah's bravery and cowardliness, the weakness of Jonah, Ruth's love and fidelity, Queen Esther's wisdom and courage, the pain of an Israelite who was captive in a foreign land, the vision and promise of Isaiah, the faithful love of Hosea, the weakness and strength of Simon Peter, the doubt and faith of Thomas, the devotion of Mary and Martha, the smallness and largeness of Paul's vision, the continuous support of Barnabas, and John's assurance of new birth and of a new world. The Gospels tell about Jesus' birth, life, teachings, miracles, death and resurrection and the establishment of his Church. Paul's letters and the rest of the New Testament are a record of the beginning of the early Church.

A HUMAN AND DIVINE BOOK

The Bible is both a human and divine book. It is human because God worked through ordinary people, using their gifts and personalities to convey his message. The Bible is divine, because God inspired persons to convey the record of how God has related to men and women in the past. It continues to be God's divine instrument to guide us in our daily living; in how we are to understand God and Jesus and live as disciples of our Lord. We acknowledge that God inspires persons not paper or parchment, and the written words of these inspired people continue to guide us in our ongoing quest to understand and serve God.

Once a mechanic was called to a famous observatory to repair one of their giant telescopes. When he took his lunch break, he sat down and read his Bible for a while. When one of the astronomers saw him doing that, he asked, "What good do you expect from that? The Bible is out of date! You don't even know who wrote it."

The mechanic paused for a moment and then observed, "Don't you make considerable use of the multiplication table in your calculations?"

"Why, yes, of course," the astronomer replied.

"Do you know who wrote them?"

"Why, no, I guess, I don't."

"Then," the mechanic asked, "how can you trust the multiplication table?"

"We trust it because, well, because it works." the astronomer responded.

"Well," the mechanic replied, "I trust the Bible for the same reason. It just works."

Through the centuries, the Bible has nourished the life of the Church. The Word of God will not fall to the ground because it is a living Word that still changes those to whom it touches today.

Rather than arguing about the Bible, it is more important to study it and learn from it. Not even the greatest biblical scholar will ever have all the insight or certain knowledge of all the original writers may have meant, but we have enough to give us authentic guidance for our spiritual knowledge. Let's draw on that knowledge.

SOME WAYS TO STUDY THE BIBLE AS AN AID TO SPIRITUAL GROWTH

I want to suggest some ways you can utilize the Bible to help you develop your spiritual life. All of these suggestions are very simple but I have found them helpful, and I believe you will too, if you put them into practice. Through the years the Bible has enriched my life and I have come to love it. I hope you will love and cherish its teachings also, if you do not already.

Read the Bible Systematically

Develop a time to study the Bible systematically and regularly. You need to set aside, as I encouraged you to do earlier, a particular time each day – whether it is morning or night – and use the time to read the Scriptures. Some people have developed a habit of randomly thumbing through the Bible to select a reading for the day without any plan or forethought. This can prove a very unproductive method for reading the Bible. Please don't go hop-skipping through the Bible or use the hunt and peck approach as your method of reading the Scriptures. That can be a very dangerous approach. Suppose your finger happens to land on the verse for the day, "The Lord has forsaken me" (Isaiah 49:14a). That's not a very good motto for the day, is it? Well, you don't like that one, so you go searching for another one. "You have turned into a debased and worthless vine"(Jeremiah 2:21b) is the next one you flip over to. Some passages will obviously be more helpful than others. Develop a regular habit of reading the Bible and don't go skipping all through its pages. Read the whole passage in its context.

Read Through a Book of the Bible

Next, learn to read one book of the Bible at a time. Select a book, like the Gospel of Mark if you have not done much reading of the Scriptures, and begin with it. Read the Gospel of Mark by beginning at the beginning and read through it in its entirety. Begin the Book of the Psalms by starting with the first Psalm and continue reading through the book until you finish it. Read at least a chapter a day. Meditate and reflect thoughtfully upon the passage. When you hop all around the Bible, you will not be able to understand its message much at all.

Suppose I took a trip overseas to visit England. Before I left, I told my grandchildren I would send them a present. Suppose what I bought for each of them was one of the Narnia Tales by C S. Lewis. When each of the three grandchildren got his or her copies, they were very confused because I had torn out some or parts of the pages of each of the books. J.T, Emily and Michael were all confused and could not read the books because of the missing and torn pages. Oh, they might make some sense of some of the lines or phrases in one place or another, but it would be so confusing and disjointed that they couldn't begin to discern Lewis' beautiful fantasies.

If you cut pages at random out of a novel by Ernest Hemingway, Mark Twain, Frederick Buechner, John Grisham or any other novelists, you couldn't make much sense out of their stories either. You would not understand their plots at all. The same result would be true in music, if you tried to play a song with only fragments of the music. It would not make sense, and you could not understand it or capture the real meaning the composer intended. Too often this is the way we read the Bible. And then we wonder why it doesn't make much sense to us. I encourage you to read the Bible a book at a time. And spend some time with each book. Move through it slowly.

Use Different Translations

Use various translations as you read the Bible. The King James Version was translated and put on the market in 1611. That is a long time ago now. The manuscripts which scholars used for that version of the Bible came from the tenth century. New Testament scholars have discovered over five thousand errors in these manuscripts which those who copied them made. In 1948, the Dead Sea Scrolls were discovered. These manuscripts were written in the first and second century. They are nine centuries older than the ones used by the King James Version. Some of the newer translations are far better, because they rely on these earlier manuscripts.

The King James Version is beautiful, but some of its words have a different meaning today. In one place a writer noted that David "prevented" the dawning of the morning. That is a pretty good act, even for David. But "prevent" in the English usage of the day meant "to come before." In another place The King James Version reads that we should be holy in our "conversation." Well, we should be, but the word "conversation" in that day didn't mean speaking – it meant "walking" or "living."

Select a translation you can understand. Translations like Good News for Modern Man, Williams, The New English Bible, The New International Version or The New Revised Standard Version are all translations which are written in today's language and are based on older manuscripts. Many people have difficulty with The King James Version today because much of it is written in a language we do not use any more. No one says, "thee," "thou," "thine," "art," "whence," and other such words. Most people cannot understand them today. Select a translation for your Bible study that is readable. Biblegateway.com is an excellent place to look at a Scripture passage in various translations.

Use Biblical Resources

Use available resources to help you to understand the Bible. When I was teaching at the seminary, a student told me all he thought he needed to preach was the Bible. "Then you are going to have some poor preaching," I responded. We all need some help in understanding the Scriptures. If you really want to be serious about your Bible study, I would suggest you invest in some good commentaries or use copies from the church library. *The New Interpreter's One-Volume Commentary on the Bible, Mercer Commentary on the Bible, Oxford Bible Commentary, Eerdmans Commentary on the Bible, New Bible Commentary*, (even older ones like) *Harper's Bible Commentary*, or *Peake's Commentary of the Bible* are excellent one volume commentaries.

William Barclay's *New Testament Daily Bible Series* is old but still excellent. The *Daily Study Bible Series* for the Old Testament by Westminster, which has been developed in Scotland and the United States, are very useful. *The Layman's Bible Commentary* by John Knox Press is older but still a helpful source for laypersons. Or The Interpretation Teaching and Preaching Series by Westminster/ John Knox Press is a good resource. If you are willing to invest more money, or can get them from your church library, you may want to consult *The New Interpreters Bible* or the new series of commentaries by Smyth & Helwys. These scholarly writings can help you understand the background of the passage and the nature of the material you are studying. These resources can help clarify the meaning of the biblical passage and set it in its proper context.

In the story recorded in the passage of Scripture from Acts Chapter 8 (Acts 8:26-36), the Ethiopian eunuch asked, "How can I understand what I am reading without some help?" How can any of us really understand the Bible without getting some help? Consult good biblical resources; use commentaries, and be willing to talk to someone else who has spent his or her life studying the Scriptures so you can learn from them.

Questions to Ask as You Read

As you read a book of the Bible be sure first of all, to set it within the context of its own day. We often move too quickly to try to discover the message it may have for our day before we have understood what its message was for the ancient world for which it was written in the first place. That is the reason we have so many strange interpretations about Revelation and Daniel. These interpreters have often not been willing to see why the writer wrote the book in the first place.

Ask questions like: What kind of literature is it? Is it prose, poetry, a parable, proverb, a letter, or a song? They are all understood in different ways. To whom was it written? Why was it written? Was this Old Testament book written to somebody from Babylon back to Jerusalem? Was it written by the Apostle Paul from a city like Ephesus to another church? What is its context? Ask the question – who, when, where, why, how, to whom? When you know its original, natural meaning, you will be able to interpret it better for our own day.

Memorize Some Scripture

I would also encourage you to memorize some of the Scripture you read each day. As you read your particular passage for the day, why not select a key verse or two to keep with you for the whole day? If you are reading where Jesus says, "I have come that you might have life and have it more abundantly," think what a marvelous passage that could be to strengthen you throughout the day. "I can do all things through Christ who strengthens me" is another powerful verse to store in our mind. In trials and tribulations think what this verse can mean. "Thy words have I hid in my heart," the psalmist said. When we have hidden Scripture in our heart, in times of need these verses can become a lamp to our feet and a light to our pathway.

Memorizing Scripture enables you to have the Bible with you at all times. The texts are stored in your mind to sustain you whenever you need them. In times of grief, pain, depression, and difficulties you can draw upon the Scriptures within your own mind, because you have spent years memorizing them.

During the Korean conflict, my first cousin was an oceanographer on the Pueblo. He was one of the two civilians who were imprisoned when the Pueblo was captured by the North Koreans. Everyone on board the Pueblo spent many months in prison. The prisoners were not allowed to have reading material of any kind – the Bible included. Richard had been brought up in church and had attended faithfully as a child and teenager. He had memorized many passages of Scripture. The men longed desperately for some inspiration. He would write verses of Scripture on toilet tissue and then, during their time in the exercise yard, he would pass the piece of paper to one of them who would, in turn, read it and pass it on to another. The words from the Bible brought them strength during a difficult time because one man had taken time to memorize Scripture passages earlier in his life. You can't do that if you have never memorized any Scripture. The practice can make the Scriptures a continuous part of your heart and mind.

Record Your Thoughts

I would also encourage you to make notes as you read the Scriptures. Jot down any thoughts or ideas that leap into your mind as you read the Bible. Make a record of what book of the Bible you are reading, what helps you are using, and the inspiration, hope, or guidance it provides you for the day. This will only take a few moments, but it can be very beneficial to you.

Read with an Open Mind

I hope you will also read the Scriptures with an open mind, expecting God's Spirit to breathe his fresh creativity upon you. Don't read it hurriedly like the morning newspaper. Read reflectively, awaiting further light from God as you journey into new biblical territory. Too often we approach the Bible assuming we know what the passage means. We need to open our minds so God's Spirit can guide us into new insights and in new directions.

Early in his life, Martin Luther had difficulty in understanding the righteousness of God. He had come to despise it. One day, as he was reading again Romans 1:17, "For in it the righteousness of God is revealed through faith for faith; as it is written, He who through faith is righteous shall live," he received fresh insight into a passage he had read hundreds of times.

"At this point I felt completely reborn, and as if I had entered paradise with its open gate. In a moment the whole meaning of Scripture seemed to have changed. Thereafter I ran through the Scriptures as if I had them in my memory, and collected analogical meanings in other words, such as the word of God, which means the work that God works in us, the virtue of God, which means the virtue through which he makes us powerful, the wisdom of God, which means the wisdom through which he makes us wise, the courage of God, the salvation of God, the glory of God. My love for that sweetest word righteousness of God was henceforth as great as my hatred for it had been hitherto. In this way this passage of Paul was truly the gate of Paradise."

It is hard to imagine what paths God could take us down, if we would be open and receptive to him. Our own narrowness and assumed knowledge often block his efforts to guide us. Let's stop assuming we already know what the Bible is saying and listen attentively to God.

Read the Bible with Imagination

I would also encourage you to read the Scriptures with imagination. I am not encouraging you to take some wild fantasy, but to try and put yourself back into that Scripture setting. If you are reading, for example, the passage where blind Bartimaeus cries, "Lord, have mercy upon me." try to see the crowd of people as they are walking by him and as they are following Jesus and listening to his teaching. See if you can envision what Bartimaeus was like. See the mob around him, pushing him back, and trying to keep him in his place. See the desperation in his face; feel his panic. Try to imagine also his sense of expectation and hope as he hears Jesus drawing near. Try to picture the scene in your mind. See also that you, like Bartimaeus, are blind and need to see. You are also crying out for Jesus to help you see. Try to see yourself within the setting so the story can address you.

Picture the setting where Moses was on a wilderness mountainside tending sheep. Try to depict the barrenness of that place. See the sheep as they are feeding nearby. In your mind's eye you may picture Moses resting as he leans against a rock. Suddenly a bush begins to burn on the mountainside. Imagine the fear, awe, and wonder that overtakes him.

Picture in your mind another occasion where a man is traveling down a road and suddenly he is attacked by robbers. See the place where it happens. Notice the isolation, his fear and panic. Imagine you are that person. See if you can get inside the story so you can see it in a different way. Are you the man who is attacked? Are you one of the passerbys or the Good Samaritan?

Let your imagination take you into the Upper Room, at the trial of Jesus, his crucifixion, at Pentecost, along with Paul on one of his missionary journeys, or with an Old Testament prophet or traveling with Jesus and listening to his teachings. Let the passage become real for you.

The Bible Reads Us

Finally, when you read the Scriptures, remember most of all that they need to read you. The Word of God comes into your life and judges you. It lifts a mirror in front of you. It brings God's Spirit before us to address our lives and show us how far removed we are from his way, the goal to which he has beckoned us to move toward, and the kind of life he wants us to live. See the mirror in the Bible which is lifted up for us to see our image. As Soren Kierkegaard has said, the Scriptures are "a letter from God with your personal address on it." See your name written in the Bible. God is speaking to you through the Bible. "Just as you do not analyze the words of someone you love, but accept them as they are said to you," Dietrich Bonhoeffer wrote, "accept the Word of Scripture and ponder it in your heart, as Mary did. That is all. That is meditation."[13]

---

13 Dietrich Bonhoeffer, *The Way to Freedom* (New York: Harper & Row, 1966), 59.

The assurance of the writer of the 23rd Psalm becomes a word of encouragement to you. The doubt of Thomas reflects your own struggle with faith. The denial of Peter reminds you of your own weakness. The disciples' request of Jesus to teach them how to pray becomes your own plea. The Bible is a timeless book. It speaks out of the life of a people from the past to speak to you today.

The Bible does not separate religion from life. Religion infuses all of life. The Bible reminds us that God searches our thoughts and knows our ways. Religion is not a subject which you can simply select or discard as you please. Genuine religion touches your life every day and requires daily commitment. "I'm not so much concerned about the part of the Bible that I don't understand," Mark Twain once said, "as those parts I do understand." What we understand of the Bible, without question, is sufficient to guide us into the abundant life. As we travel this journey of life, the Bible throws the light from its guiding beam to show us the pathway. Through his written Word, God's judgment, forgiveness, redemption, and everlasting life are made known.

During the Second World War, a chaplain was sailing on a ship with fifteen hundred Marines who were being brought back to the United States from Japan to be discharged. He received a request from some of them to have a Bible study each morning. He was surprised by their request but quickly told them that he would be glad to do it. Each morning he met with the Marines for a time of Bible study. One day they studied the passage about the raising of Lazarus from the dead. The chaplain interpreted this passage as the fulfillment of Jesus' words, "I am the resurrection and the life, if any man believes in me he will not die." Trying to drive home his point, he drew upon Dostoevsky's famous novel *Crime and Punishment*. He told them the story of Raskofnikov who had destroyed himself when he murdered another man. He was brought back to life through the reading of these words of Jesus.

After the Bible study was finished, he didn't think any great impact had been made on the men. As he was walking away from the group, one of the young soldiers walked with him and finally after struggling for a while said, "Chaplain, I felt as though every-thing we read this morning was pointed right at me. I've been living in hell for the last six months, and for the first time I feel as though I'd gotten free." He told his story about how he had gotten in real trouble while he was in occupied Japan. No one knew it but him and his sense of guilt had been so severe he did not think he could face his family back home. But that day in the Bible study his life was changed. "Until today, Chaplain," he said, "I've been a dead man. I have felt utterly condemned by myself, by my family (if they knew), and by God. I've been dead, but now, after reading about Jesus and Lazarus, I know that I am alive again. The forgiveness of God can reach out even to me. The resurrection Jesus was talking about is a real thing after all, right now."

That word comes to us from the Scriptures so we can become a new person in Jesus Christ. Read the Scriptures with the awareness they meet you and communicate the Word of God to you. Be open and responsive to that word. It is a well from which you can draw water for all of your life. It is an inexhaustible source you can never use up. Let it nourish your life. Feed upon it every day and let it help sustain you. Eat the spiritual bread it offers to fortify you for your journey through life. Search it for directions when you long for purpose in life. Let its soothing balm replenish your spirit when you are low. Draw on its healing resources when you are hurting and lonely. Trust its assurance when you doubt and lack faith. Reach out for its comfort when you are sad and grieving. Use its light as you walk through the valley of grief and death. Measure your spiritual growth by the teachings of Jesus. Bathe again and again in the pool of cleansing grace reflected in its pages. May its song give you courage on the darkest of days. Walk by the road map it offers for your Christian journey and you will find it easier to stay on the Christian way. Keep on reading its pages. Christians through the ages have found it an inexhaustible supply of wisdom and nourishment. May its words always lead you to the living Word, Jesus Christ, our Lord.

Eternal Creator, we acknowledge that too often the Bible is a closed book for us. May we be willing to open it, study it, and be nourished by it. Feed us, O Lord, through the living Word, Jesus Christ, as we study the written Word. In his strong name we pray. Amen.

CHAPTER 5

REACHING FOR THE UNATTAINABLE

A small boy was walking down the sidewalk one day and he met an even smaller boy. The larger boy had been whistling when he met the other one. The smaller lad looked up at him and asked, "Is that the best you can do?"

"Why no," the larger boy replied. Then he proceeded to prove his boast.

After he had finished, the smaller boy asked, "Why don't you do your best all the time?"

A good question for us all, isn't it? Why don't we do our best, whatever it is, all of the time?

An interesting book was written a few years ago entitled *In Search of Excellence* by Thomas Peters and Robert Waterman. With a subtitle *Lessons from America's Best-Run Companies,* this book draws conclusions from an extensive study of forty-three successful companies like Proctor and Gamble, Johnson and Johnson, Hewlett-Packard, McDonald's, and IBM. We are all interested in what makes a company excellent. How much more should we be interested in what can enable us to reach for the highest and best in our own spiritual growth.

THE QUEST FOR EXCELLENCE

In our own religious pilgrimage there is a quest, or should be, for excellence. This reach for perfection arises from a pull, motivation, urge, whisper, voice, thirst, desire or a lure for the divine. There is an inner compulsion within us to reach toward excellence – to reach for perfection.

Since the dawn of civilization men and women have been searching, seeking, and striving to know the world, themselves, and God. This search has taken them down familiar avenues at home and strange routes in foreign lands, across rugged mountains and dangerous seas, through inner struggles and mental turmoil, through agonizing groping in darkness and along lighted paths with a sense of the divine presence.

An Instinctive Pull

What is the force that motivates this pursuit of God? This quest for God seems to be instinctive. God has implanted that drive within the human soul. The psalmist expresses this feeling when he declares, "As a deer longs for flowing streams, so longs my soul for thee, O God. My soul thirsts for God, for the living God" (Psalm 42:12). "Be therefore perfect," Jesus tells his disciples, "even as your Father which is in heaven is perfect" (Matthew 5:48). A Christian of the fourth century named Augustine spoke in a similar vein. "Thou hast made us for thyself, O God, and our souls are restless until they rest in thee." The human body is so designed that water is necessary to quench its thirst. But if water did not exist, our thirst could never be satisfied and life would not be possible. Our quest for God is a desire for a spiritual necessity, which if not met, will cause us to perish spiritually, just as the lack of food or water would cause us to expire physically. This spiritual need can only be satisfied by God.

Our Quest for God

From one perspective, the Scriptures present an account of man and woman's quest for God. Many of the psalms depict the human longing to know God. "O God, thou art my God, I seek thee, my soul thirsts for thee; my flesh faints for thee, as in a dry and weary land where no water is" (Psalm 63:1). King David reminds his son, Solomon, that "if you seek him (God) he will be found by you" (I Chronicles 28:9). The prophet Amos warned Israel, "Seek the Lord and live" (Amos 5:6). Jesus also told his followers, "But seek first his kingdom and his righteousness, and all these things shall be yours as well" (Matthew 6:33).

The Scriptures portray Job's aspiration to find God's way, and also delineates the refusal of the rich young ruler to pursue his quest for eternal life when he realized the cost of discipleship. The whole history of Israel, from the time of its slavery in Egypt, the wilderness wanderings, the entrance into the Promised Land, to the captivity and dispersion, is symbolic of a nation's quest for God, who alone could give them deliverance.

God's Quest for Us

However, man and woman's longing for God arises from a prior longing of God for man and woman. The initiative lies with God. God is not some static, impassive "man upstairs," who is indifferent to the world below. He is the "Hound of Heaven" who is constantly pursuing men and women. The initial movement is from God to humanity. "In this is love, not that we have loved God but that he loved us. . ." (I John 4:10).

Throughout the Bible one reads of God's quest to covenant with men and women. God never allows individuals to set the manner or terms of his coming. God came in a "still small voice" to Elijah, he came on a mountainside to the shepherd Moses, he came "high and lifted up" to Isaiah in the temple, he came to the boy Samuel as he slep, he came to Peter in a Gentile home at Joppa, and he came to Paul on the Damascus Road. He comes in strange places and in strange ways. But he comes.

The most vivid indication of God's quest for men and women is seen in the covenant relationship he established with Israel. Human sin had separated men and women from God, but God bridged the gulf and restored communion. The covenant was God's promise of his faithfulness, which he had demonstrated in the Exodus, and the covenant was a call for the loyalty of Israel to God (Deuteronomy 7:6-9). "Now therefore, if you will obey my voice and keep my covenant, you shall be my own possession among all people; for all the earth is mine, and you shall be to me a kingdom of priests and a holy nation" (Exodus 19:5-6). The covenant was both a promise and a challenge.

THE ROAD TOWARD PERFECTION

There is a restlessness within each of us that is not satisfied until we come to rest within God. Religious writers have often described this as a search or a quest for the road toward perfection. It really seems strange, doesn't it, that human beings should speak about reaching perfection? Who among us will not acknowledge rather quickly that perfection is unattainable? It is impossible. We can't reach it.

Who can reach the standards Jesus has laid before us? He has challenged us to love our neighbors as ourselves. Do we really? We are told to love our enemies. Can we? We are instructed to keep on praying even when our prayers seem to be unanswered. Do we? We are challenged to keep on forgiving up to seventy times seven which means an unlimited number. How many do? If someone compels us to go one mile, we are told that we should be willing to go two. Jesus said we are to be perfect as our Father in heaven is perfect. At these words we want to throw up our hands and say, "I am not perfect. Look, I have a wife or husband, parents or children to attest very quickly that I am not perfect." We all know we have not attained that goal.

ETHICAL IDEALS

There are others who quickly try to dismiss all of the demands of Jesus in the Sermon on the Mount by saying that they are "merely" ethical ideals. Nobody can really live up to them. We shoot for these ideals, but we see them as unrealistic demands which we know we really can't achieve. They loom before us as what seems like impossible goals. Although we may shoot for them, strive for them, we feel they are unattainable. So let's not worry too much about them, since we know we really can't reach them.

IMPRACTICAL TEACHINGS

Others say these teachings are impractical. Loving your enemies, thinking more about somebody else than you do yourself, seeking first God's kingdom, or taking no thought for tomorrow – all of these sayings in the Sermon on the Mount seem utterly impractical. How in the world can we take them seriously? We know we are supposed to love, but deep down inside us, we really hate more than we love. We know we are supposed to be makers of peace, but we have to confess that secretively we want to be prepared in case of war. We know that we do not live up to these standards. They seem so impractical that most people do not worry about them too much. They don't want to feel guilty or experience frustration and be pulled in all directions, so they won't even think about them. They just dismiss them.

HOW TO REACH TOWARD SPIRITUAL PERFECTION

There are others, however, who take the teachings of Jesus in the Sermon on the Mount very seriously. They are envisioned as a road toward spiritual perfection. How can we achieve such a goal?

A Receding Goal

First we have to acknowledge this goal of perfection is an ever-receding one. You will never arrive at spiritual perfection. No one will make it. Luther has observed that no person is a Christian. Everyone is becoming one. No one has arrived and can declare: "I am a full-grown Christian." As the Apostle Paul wrote, "I have been saved. I am being saved, and I will be saved." We are all in the process of being saved. Jesus used the analogy of new birth. This is a point of beginning, not perfect,ion, but creation or new beginning, not ending or total fulfillment. As a Christian, we are always in the process of becoming.

You have many areas in your life where you still need to be converted, as I do in mine. There are places in your life where God hasn't been able to touch you yet. You know it, I know it, and God certainly knows it. Some of you have not begun to be converted in your pocketbook yet. Others of you have not been converted in your sex life. Many of you have not been converted from your unchristian behavior in your moral values. There are prejudices, bigotry, bad habits, and pride which have not yet been transformed. God is still working within us trying to make us whole persons. God nudges us, loves us, guides us, and motivates us – seeking to move us further along in our spiritual pilgrimage. We reach for an ever-receding goal. When we move a little closer to it, the standard also moves further beyond us. "A man's reach should exceed his grasp," Elizabeth Barrett Browning writes, "or what's a heaven for?" The goal is always beyond us, pulling us toward what we can yet be.

Fulfilling Our Purpose

The New Testament concept of perfection which Jesus refers to in Matthew 5:43-48 is derived from a Greek word which focuses on a functional concept. Perfection is not a state or condition which one has attained by his or her achievements in life. Something is perfect, in the Greek understanding, when it fulfills the purpose for which it was made. Recently I had to drill a hole through a piece of wood. I had a perfect drill. Why was it perfect? Because the hole it bored was properly done. It fulfilled its function. The New Testament word for perfect which Jesus used in this verse is a functional concept. As a Christian, you are a perfect individual when you fulfill the function for which God created you in the first place. Having been created in his image, we are to love and serve others as we have experienced his love. When we are serving him, we live the "perfect" life, because we fulfill the function for which we were created.

The Perfection of God

God is perfect, but God's perfection does not mean that God is remote and distant from us. Eduard Schweizer, the New Testament scholar, writes: "Jesus calls God perfect not because God is aloof and totally unlike man, but precisely the reverse: God is totally, undividedly devoted to man; he is faithful to his covenant; he is totally given to those he loves."[14] The command to be perfect as God our Father is perfect is understood within the context of his love. God is perfect and his love is expressed to us without reservation. He calls us to be "perfect" – to love without reservation – as we love our enemies, neighbors, and ourselves. We are to be more like him as we love.

Strength from God for the Journey

Quickly, however, you reply, "I am still not there. I can't do that. I am not strong enough. I am inadequate." Notice that those who are able to be perfect are children of God. The key word here is Father. "Be perfect like your heavenly Father." Seventeen times Jesus makes reference to Father in the Sermon on the Mount. We do not rely on our strength alone. It is not merely by my ability or my bootstrap that I am able to achieve the perfection Jesus talks about. It does not come about if I think hard enough and act right, and then I'll be able to accomplish it. We draw strength from God, our Father, who empowers us as his children to live in the world.

Jesus said, "I have come that you might have life." In him is life. "This is eternal life, that they should know you, the only true God, and whom you sent, Jesus Christ" (John 17:3). When we are attached to Christ, we experience the newness of life from his daily presence. His divine nature in us enables us "to be." He gives us strength, direction, guidance, and meaning to live up to such a high calling. We reach toward the goal, not to accomplish it by our own efforts but to acknowledge that we have been "born from above."

14 Eduard Schweizer, *The Good News According to Matthew* (Atlanta:- John Knox Press, 1977), 135.

THE PLACE OF PRAYER IN OUR QUEST

One of the things that can enable us to reach toward the New Testament sense of "perfection" is prayer. Prayer is opening yourself to God that you might sense God's presence. Bernard, an ancient Christian writer wrote these words: "Waiting upon God is not idleness but work which beats all other work to one unskilled in it." Praying is not easy. It requires discipline, time, and attention. Only those who have tried it sincerely realize the difficulty which praying can require. Private prayer is essential for spiritual growth. No one can expect to grow spiritually who does not "work" at developing the inner life. Prayer is a "journey into the heart of God." It is our attempt to press close to Christ and open our inner presence to his presence. "Prayer may be thought of as our effort simply to be open to grace," John B. Coburn writes. God is everywhere present to us; prayer is our being present to God."[15]

I want to suggest some procedures or habits that have helped me in my own prayer life. These suggestions are not original with me but are drawn from years of reading from many sources and from my own personal practice. Maybe you will find them helpful, too. Let me challenge you to try some of these suggestions this week. Maybe you can try one or more of the following on one day and see if they are useful for you. If they are helpful for a day maybe you can try them on another and see if you can begin a pattern and practice of praying at a certain time, on a certain day, in a certain place and in a certain way.

The Breath or Jesus Prayer

While sitting still inhale your breath, hold it for a moment and then exhale slowly. Repeat this several times, letting your breath in and out slowly. This practice can remind you of your desire to draw the Breath – God's Spirit – into your inner being. As you inhale and exhale your breath, you might repeat the brief phrase,

---

15 John B. Coburn, *Grace in All Things* (Boxton: Cowley Publications, 1995), 25.

"Jesus is Lord" or "Lord Jesus Christ, Son of God, have mercy on me, a sinner," or a shorter version, "Lord Jesus Christ, have mercy on me" several times. This has been called the "Jesus Prayer." Some have thought this prayer may have originated with the Desert Fathers and Mothers of the fifth century. Simply repeat the words, "Jesus is Lord" or the longer phrase again quietly or to yourself. Hopefully, after awhile you will begin to focus your mind and spirit on sensing Christ's presence. Other phrases you might repeat are the following: "Lord, have mercy." Holy Spirit, breathe on me." "Jesus is my peace." "Creator God, continue to create in me." This repetition may last for only a few moments or it can be extended for a lengthy period of time or, as some believe, this prayer can be prayed continually even in one's working or sleeping. Allow it to bring you inner calm and relaxation as you open yourself to God.

Henri J. M. Nouwen writes that the "Jesus Prayer," "Lord Jesus Christ, have mercy on me" offers a powerful summary of all prayer:

It directs itself to Jesus, the son of God, who lived, died and was raised for us; it declares him to be the Christ, the anointed one, the Messiah, the one we have been waiting for; it calls him our Lord, the Lord of our whole being: body, mind and spirit, thought, emotions and actions; and it professes our deepest relationship to him by a confession of our sinfulness and by a humble plea for his forgiveness, mercy, compassion, love and tenderness.[16]

Centering Prayer

Centering prayer has its origin in the Trappist monks' use of the anonymous writing entitled The Cloud of the Unknowing. This practice invites one to become quiet and seek to center – rest – "in" God and focus on the One who is the source of our creation. This is an attempt to reconnect with the spiritual Center of the universe. You are seeking to enter the inner "cave" of your being. Our time of praying is a desire to be exposed to Christ and to spend time gazing on his presence and to be transformed by that presence. Is this not

16 Henri J. M. Nouwen, *Reaching Out: The Three Movements of the Spiritual Life* (New York: Doubleday, 1986), 146.

what Paul was writing about Christ when he declared, "We are being transformed into the same likeness as himself, passing from one glory to another" (2 Corinthians 3:18, Moffatt).

As you become quiet yourself, lift one word into the center of your thoughts like peace, hope, love, grace, Christ, mercy, forgiveness or light. Repeat it again and again as you center your mind on God. As you pray silently, if you become distracted and your mind moves away from your focus on God to some other matter, like a personal concern, needs, what happened yesterday or might happen tomorrow, some task to be done, a family problem, or how to organize something, etc, come back in your centering thoughts to your chosen one word and continue repeating it again. The constant repetition of this one word can help you focus your mind and thought on God. This can be like turning on a light in a dark room while reading a book. As long as you have a light, you can focus on your book and read. In a similar way, centering provides a "light" in your darkness to focus your mind on Christ.

I have found this form of praying also very useful at night, if I am having trouble going to sleep or simply as a means to help me relax as I lie down to sleep with my last "centering" being on God. I simply repeat over and over silently to myself a word like "rest," "peace," or "trust." I often find that soon I have drifted off into sleep and did not know when I ceased to repeat the word.

Ingathering

Get up early one morning, or choose some convenient time during the day, and spend five minutes in silence with God. Do nothing. Don't pray. Don't read the Scriptures. Don't verbalize anything. Just be silent. Listen. Sit still for five minutes and wait before God. Mystics call this "in gathering." Wait silently before God so that God can meet you. Use this time to listen to God. We often spend too much time talking when we pray and very little time listening. Spend some time again simply listening.

Some monks and nuns take vows of silence and obedience. The word obedience is derived from a Latin word, obaudire, which means to listen with intense attentiveness. Audire is to listen or to hear. The word for deaf is absurdus. When we do not listen to God we are absurd – deaf. Genuine praying involves listening. Devote some time to silence and seek to tune your ears to listen for the "sound" of the voice of God in the sounds of silence. "A man prayed, and at first he thought that prayer was talking," noted Soren Kierkegaard. "But he became more and more quiet until in the end he realized that prayer is listening."[17]

Meditate on a Scripture Text

After you have spent some time in the Breath Prayer or Centering Prayer or Ingathering or in silence, whether you have spent five minutes, fifteen minutes, or longer, you might want to then select a passage from the Scriptures to read. You may already be following a reading plan or want to read some selected passages from the Psalms, or portions of the Gospel of John or some other passage you have in mind. At this stage, do not use commentaries or other devotional helps.

Read the Scriptures. Read and reflect on your text. Muse over it. Find the theme of the passage and tune into that emphasis and repeat the theme over to yourself again and again. You may find a verse you can memorize for your daily "watch word." Think of the spiritual strength you can carry through the day with words like "I can do all things through Christ" (Philippians 4:13). Or "I have come that you might have life and have it more abundantly," says Jesus (John 10:10). Words like this can be mediated upon, memorized and used as a source of strength for the day.

Focused Prayer

After your time of silence and biblical mediation, you may then want to spend some time in focused prayer. Offer your prayer of adoration for God and God's divine mercy. Express your gratitude for God's blessings. Confess your sins and ask God for forgiveness.

17 Soren Kierkegaard, *Christian Discourses*, Trans. Walter Lowie (Oxford: Oxford University Press, 1940), 59.

Be honest and specific in your confession. Remember this is between you and God and God already knows. We can't pretend or
play games with God.

Then lay your requests before God. Again, be specific. Pray
for your own needs and for God's guidance as you seek to serve
Christ and minister in his name. Offer intercessory prayers for the
concerns and needs of your family and others whom you know in
your church, community or on a national level.

Lectio Divina

Lectio Divina (divine reading) is a much more consecrated
focus on the Scriptures for meditation than the above. Some believe
that this is perhaps the oldest form of Christian meditation. One
usually selects a passage of Scripture, following a Lectionary reading
for the day, or from one's own choosing. This "Divine Reading"
normally follows four steps. First (lectio), one reads the text very
slowly and carefully. Second (meditation), the reader focuses their
thoughts on what the passage says about God and how that particular passage relates to the reader's own life. Third (oratio), the person
meditating then seeks to respond in prayer to the passage he or she
is reading. Sometimes the reader focuses on his or her breathing as
one strives to be "silent" before God. Fourth (contemplatio), the
person silently listens for God to speak to him or her through the
Holy Spirit. The purpose is not to read a large portion of Scripture
but to focus instead on a text until one has exhausted its meaning
even reading it over again and again. This meditation cannot be
done quickly but requires a longer time of hallowed attention.

Reflect on the Prayers of Others

I have found it helpful to read and reflect on the written prayers
of others in my own devotional life. I have sometimes drawn on
those persons some have designated as saints like St. Benedict,
Francis of Assassi, Ignatius of Loyola and the Desert Fathers. I
have also found useful the printed prayers of persons like Robert
Raines' *Lord, Could You Make It a Little Better*, John Baillie's *A Di-*

ary of Private Prayer, Walter Rauschenbusch's *Prayers for the Social Awakening*, Catherine Marshall's *The Prayers of Peter Marshall*, and others by John Killinger, Charles Wesley, Harry Emerson Fosdick, Joyce Rupp and many more.

I have also found it helpful to draw on the prayers of the psalmists and to voice them as my own prayer. There is an endless supply, of course. You might want to use Psalm 1, 4, 8, 19, 22, 23, 28, 30, 38, 51, 55, 67, 96, 100, 131, 146, or 150. Read the psalms for yourself and find a psalm which reflects your particular need for that day and let it help you pray your prayer. This can be a rewarding experience.

Another supportive tool is to pray The Lord's Prayer and then reflect on each phrase of it. This can enable us to focus on the major spiritual themes of our lives. I have written a little book entitled *The Lord's Prayer Today* which you might find helpful in this practice.

The Trust Prayer

Through all our praying there has to be an awareness of our need ultimately to trust in God. We voice our prayers to God or listen silently for God's directions or answer to our prayers. Having prayed to God, then we need to quietly to await God's response. Someone has suggested our prayers in which we express our worries, fears, problems, concerns, grieving, burdens, hopes, aspirations, longings, etc should be placed in a prayer "box" called the SFGTD box – Something For God To Do box. This means we can express our anger, fears, sighs, uncertainties, anxieties, frustrations or whatever to God with the assurance that God does not reject nor not listen to us because of these feelings. We offer our prayers to God and then leave them to God to answer in his own way and not in our own way. The Scriptures remind us of this in so many places. "Trust in the Lord with all your heart and do not lean on your own understanding" (Proverbs 3:5). This, of course, is easier said than done. Yet, it is the way of the obedient life.

Make a Beginning

If you are able to begin and continue the practices mentioned above, you will slowly begin to build into your life an avenue for God to minister to you. Open your inner self and invite God's presence into the depths of your own innermost self. But you will not find that easy. Begin by trying to meditate or pray for a few minutes. To attempt a long period of time when one is not used to devoting any time to prayer is not the best way to begin. Five minutes for some people will seem like an eternity! Thirty minutes of Bible study, reflection, and prayer will seem like a long period of time when you have never done it. Try to open your spirit to God in this way, and maybe you can slowly begin to build a meaningful prayer relationship with him. It is a spiritual journey which is worthy of all of our efforts.

The Importance of Worship

As essential as personal and private prayer and mediation are for our spiritual development, corporate worship is also very important. If you are going to reach toward inner spiritual development, worship is an absolute essential. It cannot be an occasional affair. It has got to be an ongoing openness of yourself to God. Vital worship cannot be an occasional drop-in affair before God, but requires a week-after-week commitment to seeking his presence in church. In the beauty of many sacred places, you and I can worship even if the choir is off key or if the minister delivers the world's biggest sermonic bomb. You can still sit in church and meditate and sense the power and presence of God. Worship is essential, it is not optional.

A Russian university student spoke to a student friend, "You Christians are all right except on one point. You seem to think that if a person believes in Christ, he has to join a church. I am a believer, but I don't belong to the church." The American Christian responded: "Suppose you and I were the only Christians in this city, and each should hear that the other professes Christ. Do you know what we would do, if we were real believers? The first thing we would do would be to look each other up and begin talking. Soon we would be praying together, studying together, and devising means to win others to Christ, and so on. That is what a church is. You don't have to join a church. You do so because Christ is in your heart."

GIVING IS ESSENTIAL

On your road of spiritual pilgrimage, you will discover that giving is essential. I'm not referring here primarily to money, though it certainly is a part of the total picture. The stewardship of our financial resources, of course, should reflect our commitment to God. For a person to become a Christian and cling to selfishness is to misunderstand the faith. Any person, who has really understood the gospel of Christ and experienced the power of his redemption cannot be a parasite and feed on others. Only a parasite takes from others without giving something in return. Christ has forgiven us of our sins and has challenged us to find ways and means of ministering in his name and leading others to experience his redeeming grace.

As a Christian, having received so much, we want to give out of our vast riches and share the love we have known with others. We need to find ways to give ourselves in ministry to helping others, like visiting the sick or grieving, or working in a food kitchen to feed the poor or finding a place of service in one's own church, or going on a mission trip to assist other persons who may be in need in our own country or in some foreign land.

THREE CAUTION SIGNS

We are Not Perfect

As you walk down the road of spiritual perfection, try to remember three things. Remember, first of all that you and I are not perfect. We are all in pilgrimage. We are still in the midst of our failures, sins, inadequacies, and all of our limitations. We are all in various stages of beginning. "We do not want to be beginners," Thomas Merton observed. "But let us be convinced of the fact that we will never be anything else but beginners, all our life!"[18] But this does not mean God does not love us. He is present with us, wherever we are, and is seeking to guide us further down the spiritual trail. Whether we are strong or weak, bright or dull, well or ill, God loves us and wants to help us advance in our spiritual journey.

Grace Crawford wrote about a young boy named Michael who could hardly move in his wheelchair when she first met him. This severely handicapped boy was not able to talk or use his arms or legs. She saw him several months later, and he had made some slight progress. His eyes seemed to be more alert and he seemed happier. About a year later when she saw him, Michael was bright-eyed with enthusiasm. He only needed his wooden wheelchair when he had to travel a long distance. He could sit in a chair, and he could move his hands slightly. And what he couldn't say, because his speech was so slurred, he could pen in a crude handwriting.

She watched Michael as he sat before his small wooden frame where he was weaving something. He reached over and hugged it before he began his day's work. He was rejoicing in what he had been able to accomplish so far. His weaving was going to be a potholder. So far his potholder was absolutely perfect. He had not made a mistake in it. It was to be a gift for his mother. When Grace came over to speak to Michael that day, he tried to tell her something, but she could not understand him. So, he took a pencil and wrote in a scribbled hand across the page, "I am proud of myself."[19] He had found dignity.

Out of divine love, God affirms us. As a Christian, we acknowledge that we are immature or childlike in our faith no matter how

---

18 Thomas Merton, *Contemplative Prayer* (Garden City, NY: Doubleday, 1969), 37.

19 Robert A Raines, *Soundings* (New York: Harper & Row, 1970), 18-19.

long we have been a Christian or how much we may have studied or grown spiritually. We are still amateurs in knowing God in all of God's divine fullness. Nevertheless, God loves us unconditionally. We are not yet fully whole, but God loves us and continues to guide us as we reach for spiritual maturity. We can know spiritual joy as we move forward a step in our pilgrimage to be more like God.

The Christian Way Is Difficult

Second, remember the Christian way is difficult. Jesus never said it was easy. The call to reach upward to be like God is a goal or standard that is always unattainable. We realize we can never really be like God. All of our lives we will pattern our lives after Jesus Christ and seek to be like God the Father. This goal is unattainable, but we reach toward it. Jesus never did hide the flint edge in his call to discipleship. He always told his followers it was costly to follow him. "If any man will come after me, let him deny himself," Jesus said, "and take up his cross and follow me." The rich young ruler, who felt he had fulfilled the Jewish laws and traditions, asked, "What must I do to be perfect?"

"Go and sell all you have," Jesus responded, "and come follow me." His demands reached beyond anything that ruler ever imagined.

And so it is for us. In the shop, on the playground, at school, home, or wherever we are, Jesus Christ stands at our elbows directing and motivating us in all we say and do. This means Jesus Christ will not permit other things to crowd him out. He demands the center of our lives. He will not let the trivialities of our lives push him out. He demands the central place. Too many of us want to keep him only on the edges of our lives. But he demands first place. "Seek first the Kingdom of God," he commands. This does not mean seek it after everything else has been satisfied, but seek first the Kingdom of God – not your family, not your friends, not your ambitions, not wealth or fame – but his Kingdom.

We sometimes sing, "All to Jesus I Surrender." How can we sing that? We have not begun to surrender all! Some of us haven't even given God a small place in our life, much less all. Can you sing with meaning, "All to Jesus – my total life I give him?"

One night a visitor, at one of my former churches, spoke to me about what the worship service meant to her. 'Unlike some people who have been Christians for a long time," she observed, "my husband and I are new Christians. We are still excited about being a Christian." Her words struck as an indictment on the way many of us live as Christians. We have lost our enthusiasm for the faith. The joy, radiance, and wonder of the gospel have grown pale in our minds. The Christian way is no longer the central thrust of our life. Our zeal has cooled. Our religion takes a back seat to everything else. But Christ says, "I must have first place in your life, if I really mean anything to you."

Build on Your Present Faith

Finally, learn to build on the faith you have. None of us share the exact same place in his or her spiritual pilgrimage. All of us are at different levels, because we have come in at separate times, and in various ways, and at different places. As we grow in our awareness of Christ and his way, we have to build on the faith we have. Jesus reminded us, "If you have faith like a grain of mustard seed you can say to that mountain, 'Move from here to there,' and it will move and nothing will be impossible for you" (Matthew 17: 20). Jesus was using an exaggerated image to suggest what a small amount of faith could accomplish.

Do you know how grass grows on the desert's edge? It builds on the edge of the grass already there and slowly extends its life a little bit further. In our spiritual life we build on the edge of the faith we already have. As we build on this faith, our faith slowly advances further, building on our present foundation. Quit saying, "Oh, when I do this, or when I am this age, or when I have studied this, or when I have accomplished that – I will be able to believe." Begin where you are.

I read about a small man who was admiring the powerful muscles of a large man. The small, scrawny man kept saying: "Boy, if I were as big as you are, I'd go into the forest and get me the biggest bear and I'd tear him limb to limb." Finally the big man could stand it no longer. "Son," he replied, "there are a lot of little bears out there in the woods."

Start where you are. Start with the problems in your life. Build on your growing edge, move forward, develop the faith you have. Open your life to God and grow. You don't think you have thirty minutes a day you can give to prayer? Give five. You can't find five. Give one minute to prayer and devotion. Then that minute, hopefully, will grow to two, and then three and so on. Learn to open your life to God, move one small inch at the time. Jesus has called us to move beyond where we are, to reach for the unattainable. He always challenges us to reach higher and further. We are to be like God. We know we will never realize this goal, but it is the challenge he has put before us. Reach for it. Don't give up. Reach!

You may be concerned because you haven't grown in your faith. It's like you have been holding onto the reins. Psalm 4:7 confesses our feeling when the writer declares, "Deep calls out to deep." Let go and let God have control of your life. Your personal spiritual life may seem superficial, and you long for a deeper experience. Invite God to come into the inner caverns of your life. Throw open the door and let God into the depths of your inner being. Be warmed and nurtured by his presence. Move out of the path of the noise, rushing and crowds around you into a quiet place and lay open your soul like freshly plowed soil for the "rain" of God's grace upon your life.

Some of us may need to let God lead us into a higher understanding of what it means to be a Christian in our business life, home life, and recreational life. Let God come into your life and move you toward what God has created you to be. You are his son or daughter. You are God's child. Let God love you with divine grace, and then go forth and love as you have been loved.

Oh, Loving Creator, we thank you for your love which is beyond our understanding. Having been loved so much by your great love, may we now seek to reach out and love others as we have experienced your redeeming grace. Through our Lord's powerful name, we pray. Amen.

CHAPTER 6

WHEN YOU CAN'T PRAY ANYMORE

Return with me now to our concern about unanswered prayer. Listen to others who have voiced concerns about feeling that God has not responded to their prayers. For several weeks I had visited a woman who was seriously ill in the hospital. Her husband walked with me into the hall one day and exclaimed, "Pastor, I simply can't pray anymore. Ann's illness has drained me of all my strength."

A couple turned to me one day in another hospital and said, "We have prayed so hard for our child, but we have had no response at all from God. Tommy continues to get sicker and sicker. Heaven seems simply to be made of brass. Why does God not answer?"

A woman who had been deeply depressed for several months said to me one day, "There is no point in praying. I can't feel anything anymore. I don't know if God cares or even if there is a God. I have such a void and absence of his presence in my life."

All of these persons were faithful, active church members. Their feelings are not uniquely their own. Sometimes you and I have known these kinds of struggles when we have sat by beds of those who were ill or have stood by the grave of a loved one. Or we have had similar feelings when we have been depressed, or without a job, or had some kind of frustrating experience. We, too, have known the feeling when heaven seemed to be deaf. The door to God's presence seemed shut. Our knock brought no response – no indication of any kind that there was a God who hears or cares.

Lessons from Matthew 15:21-28

The story found in the fifteenth chapter of the Gospel of Matthew (15:21-28) is not directly on prayer; yet it is. Maybe we can learn some lessons from that story about praying when it seems difficult. Note the setting of the story. Jesus had taken a trip which carried him about thirty miles above the northern border of Galilee into Gentile territory. It is uncertain exactly why Jesus traveled to Tyre and Sidon. Some scholars have indicated that Jesus may have traveled there to flee from Herod who wanted to put an end to the ministry of this itinerant preacher. That could be true. Others have speculated that Jesus may have gone there for some quiet time and rest.

Whatever his reason for being there, Jesus wanted the knowledge of his presence kept a secret. He did not want the fact he was there spread around. Evidently that was impossible. It is at this point the woman in our biblical story enters the scene. She had a sick child at home. She had heard the word a Jewish rabbi who had healing power was in town. She threw caution to the wind, and even knowing the attitude of the Jewish people toward Gentiles, came rushing to the edge of the crowd following Jesus and screamed to him for help. I believe this story can provide some pointers for us when it is difficult to pray or our prayers seem to be unanswered.

Apparently, No Response

Notice, first of all, that Jesus was silent to the woman's cry. He did not answer her with a single word (15:23). His heart seemed frozen toward her. There was not the usual compassionate ouflowing of love toward her as he had indicated toward others who came along his path. His hand did not reach out to touch the sick child. He gave no word of hope – no response at all.

Unrealistic Expectations of Prayer

Why? Well, we are not certain, are we? Jesus was certainly a stranger to this woman. And she really did not know him. In a similar manner many persons go rushing into God's presence. God is a stranger to them, yet they expect God to grant whatever prayer they pray. Their prayers may be selfish, egotistical, foolish, or even absurd. Nevertheless, they expect God to respond instantly to their request.

As I indicated earlier sometimes we have some strange notions about prayer. Some people view praying like putting coins in a candy machine. Just as we get our choice of candy from a vending machine by inserting coins, many think we can say our prayer and we should expect to get an immediate response to suit our wishes. Whatever I want, God is supposed to supply it. I express my desire, and wait for God to respond. To a sweet, grandfather figure, the cries go up, "Gimmie this or gimmie that!" Is that really a biblical understanding of praying?

Many of us are like the small boy who was depicted in a cartoon praying, "Aunt Stella isn't married yet. Uncle Herbert hasn't got a job. Daddy's hair is still falling out. I'm tired of saying prayers for this family without getting results!"

There are a lot of us who feel the same way. We want results when we pray. We assume our wish is a demand which God is supposed to meet.

In *Children's Letters to God*, a small boy expresses the kinds of prayer which too many of us pray. He writes: "Dear God, I would like these things: A new bicycle, a number three chemistry set, a dog, a movie camera, and a first baseman glove. If I can't have them all, I would like to have most of them. Yours truly, Eric." Prayer for many of us is our "wish list" before God.

Sin Hinders Our Prayers

Sometimes God is silent to our prayers because of our sin. Sin can block our pathway to God. It is difficult to pray when we harbor secret sin. Jesus taught us when we pray to remember to say, "Hallowed be thy name." We are to remember the holiness of God. Unconfessed sin can separate us from God. Sometimes God's silence is a rebuke to the sin within us that we need to confess. We pray to be purged of all secret sins.

Even the Devout Sometimes Experience Silence

But there are times even deeply devout persons find it is difficult to pray. God is no stranger to them. They have prayed often in times of joy, happiness, and have worshiped faithfully. Yet now they seem to feel only silence before God. If you and I have experienced times of God's silence in our prayer life, remember we join the ranks of some of the great saints. Jeremiah had prophesied the destruction of Jerusalem and he had to sit alone, rejected, and misunderstood. Out of a broken spirit, he prayed, "God, you are like a deceitful brook that in the spring of the year has water. But in the dry season there is nothing there. You are like a wadi to me. I have prayed to you and I get no response (Jeremiah 15:18)." The psalms are filled with pains, agonies, and sobs of those who wanted to know where God was in their moments of hurt and need.

Martin Marty, in his book, *A Cry of Absence*, which was written after the death of his wife from an extended battle with cancer, discusses the "dark night of his soul." He turned to the book of Psalms for consolation and discovered those who thought the psalms focused primarily on praise and the call for an ever-present smile, had not read them carefully. Marty observes:

To my surprise, I noticed that more than half of the psalms had as their major burden or context life on the wintry landscape of the heart. Many more contained extensive reference to the spiritual terrain of winter, even if it did not predominate. Only about a third of the psalms were, indeed, the simple property of those for whom the summery style would exhaust Christian spiritually.[20]

The Bible Denotes Times of God's Silence

The psalms depict the cries of men and women in pain, loneliness, and agony who wonder where God is in their time of distress.

20 Martin E. Marty, *A Cry of Absence* (San Francisco: Harper & Row, 1983), 83.

Then look at Job's agonizing plea, "Oh, that I knew where I might find him (Job 23:3)." The Apostle Paul prayed to God three times to remove his thorn in the flesh, but it was not to be (2Corinthians 12:8-9). Jesus prayed in the Garden of Gethsemane that his cup of suffering might pass. It did not (Matthew 27:46). Later hanging on a cross, he cried, "My God, my God, why have you forsaken me?" (Matthew 27:46). Some of the most devout persons have felt a sense of aloneness and the silence of God.

Prayer Is Not Magic

Many assume prayer is a sort of "magical tool" that can be used to get whatever they want from God. Mark Twain's Huckleberry Finn gives us a picture of this magical attitude toward prayer. Huck had been told by Miss Watson that if he prayed for anything he could get it. When he discovered praying did not produce results in the way he wanted, he quit praying.

"Miss Watson," Huck said, "she took me in the closet and prayed, but nothing came of it. She told me to pray everyday, and whatever I asked for I would get. But it warn't so. I tried it. Once I had fish-line, but no hooks. It warn't any good to me without hooks. I tried for hooks three or four times, but somehow I couldn't make it work. By and by, one day I asked Miss Watson to try it for me, but she said I was a fool. She never tole me why, and I couldn't make it out no way. . . I says to myself, if a body can get anything they pray for, why don't Deacon Winn get back the money he lost on pork? Why can't the widow get back her silver snuff box that was stole? Why can't Miss Watson fatup? No, says I to myself, there ain't nothin' in it."[21]

There are a lot of folks who have come to that conclusion about prayer.

---

21 Mark Twain, *The Adventures of Huckleberry Finn* (New York: Rinehart and Co., Inc.,1916), 10-11.

The Importance of Persistence

Jesus was silent to her request. But look further. The woman persisted. She persisted in expressing her need. Luke noted that Jesus taught his disciples in parables "to show that they should keep on praying and never lose heart" (Luke 18:1). In these parables, Jesus told about a woman who went to a judge and continued to hound him until he responded. The other parable was about a man who went to his neighbor's house at midnight and knocked on his door after the man had gone to bed and awakened him to ask for food. Jesus tells us, "Ask, seek, knock" (Luke 11:9-11). Literally, Jesus encouraged us to keep on knocking, keep on asking, and keep on seeking. Do not give up. As Paul entreated, we are to "pray without ceasing" (1 Thessalonians 5:17). Pray until your knuckles are bloody from knocking at God's door.

Some of us may pray once or twice and, because we do not get what we want immediately as we pray, we assume that God is not listening, so we give up. Think what our life would be like in other areas if that is the way we acted.

I'm not into snow skiing at all. Our son is and he loves it. Suppose I decide one cold day that I would go to some majestic peaks to ski. After getting my skis on, I start down the slope for the first time. As I try to ski, I might fall down two or three times or more. I might even break a leg. I could throw the skis aside and declare, "This proves skiing is no good and it doesn't work!" But the fault is not in skiing, is it? The fault lies in my unwillingness to try but once or twice. There are many of us who take that kind of approach in praying. We tried it but didn't get the results we wanted.

Extended Prayer Time

For those of us who do pray, our prayer time may be very brief. We read or hear about the great saints of Christendom who spend hours in prayer and wonder, "What could they possibly do all this time? I can't pray for more than a couple of minutes and then my

prayer time is over. I don't know what they do to fill up the time."
We all understand that struggle, don't we?

A great saint was asked one day what he did during his extensive time of prayer each day. "I simply sit," he replied, "and I look at God and he looks at me." Listening can often be one of the most powerful ways of praying. Sometimes we need to stop talking or doing anything and pause to listen to God. P. T. Forsyth, an English theologian, wrote:

To cultivate the ceaseless spirit of prayer, use more frequent acts of prayer. To learn to pray with freedom, force yourself to pray. The great liberty begins in necessity.

Do not say, "I cannot pray. I am not in the spirit." Pray till you are in the spirit. Think of analogies from lower levels. Sometimes when you need rest most you are too restless to lie down and take it. Then compel yourself to lie down, and to lie still. Often in ten minutes the compulsion fades into consent, and you sleep, and rise a new man.[22]

Do not lose heart. Even when God is silent, persist.

A Hard Response

Although the woman persisted, she didn't get the answer from Jesus which she wanted. Look at the harshness of the reply of Jesus. "I have come only to the house of Israel" (15:24). He reminded her and his disciples that he had come to fulfill the covenant relationship which God had made to bring his salvation to the nation of Israel. But his next words are even more severe. "It is not right to take the children's bread and throw it to the dogs." Even if one notes the Greek means little dogs or pet dogs that eat the scraps around the table and is not a reference to wild dogs, this does not remove the sting.

No matter how you look at these words, they are still words of degradation. It is a harsh rebuke that comes to her. This bread is a reference to the leftovers which those eating at the table would

---

22 P.T. Forsyth, *The Soul of Prayer* (Grand Rapids: Wm. Eerdmans Co., 1916), 62.

use to wipe food or grease off their fingers. They didn't have cloth or paper napkins in those days but used pieces of leftover bread for that purpose. After wiping their fingers on the bread, they threw it on the floor and the pet dogs came along and ate it.

God Responds in Different Ways than Expected

God does not always respond the way we want, does he? Sometimes God's answer seems harsh. I suggested earlier that if God always granted our prayers in the way we ask them, we would really not get the sincere desire we wanted. I read of a pilot who had to abandon his plane and parachute to safety. He watched his plane crash into the ocean. He landed safely on a small island. He built himself a lean-to shelter and prayed for help. One day his fire got out of control and burned down the small lean-to which he had built. He began to curse his circumstances and felt his situation was hopeless. But a ship came to his rescue because they had seen the fire from his lean-to and knew someone was there.

If God always granted us exactly what we asked for, I wonder what kind of shape we would really be in. We don't always know what is best for ourselves. As small children, we may have prayed to God that we might be rock singers, space pilots, basketball players and the like. Fortunately, our parents guided us to more realistic goals. God also knows how childish many of our requests are.

Continue Praying

Many do not like the answers they get from God and decide to give up on prayer. I read about a British scientist in India who became concerned about the Hindu practice of drinking the polluted water from the sacred river, Ganges. He persuaded a Hindu priest to go down to the river with him. He thought he could convince the priest to influence his people not to drink the water when he saw all of the impurities in it. He put a sample of the water under his microscope to reveal the impurities in the water. The priest looked through the microscope and saw all of the crawling, harmful life bubbling within the water. What was his response? He smashed the microscope!

Some of us pray to God, and we have in mind the answer we want. When the response we expect does not come, we reject God. Rather than respond by a change in our way of living, or react differently toward others, we turn away from God. Prayer should not be seen as a means of getting our own way but as a way of allowing God to show us what God desires for us. Our goal should not be to see if we can get our way but instead to discover the will of God for our life. We ought to strive not to try to change God's mind but to align our mind with God's way as best as we can determine it. "And this is the judgment, that the light has come into the world, and people loved darkness rather than the light" (John 3:19 NRSV).

Listen with Humility

Notice the woman's response to the words of Jesus. "Yes, Lord, yet . . . even the dogs eat the crumbs that fall from their master's table (15:27)." What humility! She is willing to be addressed as a dog if God will grant her request. In utter humility she comes to Christ and persistently says, "True, Lord, yet the dogs eat the scraps from the table." A "crumb" from the Master's table is enough. She acknowledges first his mission to Israel, but believes even a "crumb" from his table to one like her who is a "dog," inferior as she might be, allows her to share in the blessings of the household. Through faith, persistence, and humility, she reveals the depth of her trust.

A Great Faith

Hearing this Jesus exclaims, "Woman, great is your faith! Let it be done for you as you wish" (15:28). At that moment her child was healed. This was the first woman outside Israel who responded to Christ. She was the second Gentile to whom Jesus had commended for their great faith. The centurion was the first. Initially, it seemed she would not get any response from Jesus, but through persistent faith, she received the blessing she desired.

WE CANNOT ALWAYS UNDERSTAND GOD'S WAYS

We can never fully understand God's ways. They are beyond us. A small child whose father is a surgeon cannot understand why his father cuts on people. The child does not understand that a surgeon may have to "cut" people to make them well. Likewise, a small child whose father is an architect may look at the designs of a twenty story building and not understand them. They are beyond the small child's comprehension. As high as the heavens are above the earth, God's ways are beyond us. We can never understand all of God's ways or the working of God's universe, or even what is best for us, but we can come in humble trust like the Gentile woman and say, "True, Lord, yet I trust you, and I give my life to you." Sometimes God grants the desires of our heart and at other times God remains silent. On this occasion, the woman got what she wanted. But we may not. Even when we do not, like Paul we say, "His grace is sufficient" (2 Corinthians 12:9).

When Daniel Poling was a young man, he was called home from a summer camp because his brother was seriously ill from typhoid. On discovering his brother's condition, he was not greatly disturbed because he had wonderful experiences in prayer and felt confident. With a sense of assurance, he went into a room next door to his brother's room and prayed. He soon felt his prayers were getting nowhere. He felt no answer and began to be angry and feel despair. "I wanted the life of my brother more than anything else on earth, so much that I was ready to pledge my own life against his recovery," Poling said. "But there was no answer, no slight intimation that I had ever been heard."

He went outside the house and took a long walk. When he returned, he found his brother was weaker. He finally fell asleep from exhaustion. He awoke at down and found his prayer had been answered, but it was not the answer he wanted. His younger brother was dead. But strangely with that wrong answer, he received peace and power. From that experience he got "power that was," he said, "never to leave me, in sickness and health, through war and peace, at the birth and at the dying." Peace came to him that lasted through all of his life, even the tragic loss of his own son during the war when the ship he was on sank. He did not get the answer he wanted but through his unanswered prayer, he received an answer that gave him inner peace.

As we remain open to God, we can follow God's leadership whenever God guides us. Remaining receptive, we are open to God's spirit and can walk in the light of God's presence. We remember the condition which Jesus placed on his assurance to answer our prayers: "If you abide in me, and my words abide in you" (John 14:14; 15:7). Always we pray, "Not my will but thine be done."

David Redding has expressed the inner feeling of many of us in his prayer entitled, "If I Could Pray Again."

> "If I could pray
> Again,
> I think I would begin
> The way my mother Taught me –
> Beside my bed.
> But when I lay me
> Down,
> I find I can't go back:
> The bridge is burned.
> I can't go on like this:
> The road ahead dead-ends.
> My only hope is height.
> And yet
> I know of nothing new
> For that, my Father,
> Except to try once more –
> Just as I used to do –
> Asking inspiration
> In this more pressing
> Situation;
> Remembering You promised

The Kingdom
To those becoming
Like little children once again.
And so I pray You, Lord,
Once more;
Teach me this time My soul to keep
For others' sake,
As well as Christ's.
O let me sleep
And wake tonight
On that,
'Till prayer comes back
To me.
Amen.[23]

In my life I have learned I must trust God. God knows what is best. I am thankful God has not always answered all of my prayers just as I have prayed them. I have learned I have to live in cooperation with God's moral laws and the laws of the universe. I have learned God doesn't expect me to pray for him to do something for me that I can do myself. I have learned not to base God's presence with me on how I feel. Even when I don't sense his presence, God is still present. God is always present even when God is silent. But pray, I must. It is the air that enables my soul to breathe.

O God, at times you do seem to be silent to my prayers. I want to sense your divine presence. Help me to know that even your silence discloses your abiding presence with me. Help me to trust you even when the way is uncertain, confusing, difficult or demanding. Breathe through my breath each moment as I open my spirit to your loving Spirit. Amen.

---

23 David A. Redding, *If I Could Pray Again* (New York: Fleming H. Revell Co., 1965), 15-16.

A SUGGESTED
BIBLIOGRAPHY

(The following books have been helpful to me in my spiritual journey. Some of these books are no longer in print but can be located in used bookstores or online. They are worth the effort.)

Appleton, George, general editor. *The Oxford Book of Prayers*. Oxford: Oxford University Press, 1989.

Baillie, John. *A Diary of Private Prayer*. New York: Charles Scribner's Sons, 1949.

Baillie, John. *A Diary of Readings*. New York: Charles Scribner's Sons, 1955.

Barclay, William. *Daily Celebration*. Waco: Word Books, 1971.

_____. *Everyday Prayers*. New York: Harper & Row, 1959.

_____. *The Plain Man's Book of Prayers*. London: Collins, 1959.

Bondi, Roberta C. *To Pray and to Love*. Minneapolis: Fortress Press, 1991.

Bonhoeffer, Dietrich. *Life Together*. New York: Harper & Row, 1954.

Bourgeault, Cynthia. *Centering Prayer and Inner Awakening*. Cowley Publications, 2004.

Cameron, Julia. *Answered Prayers: Love Letters from the Divine*. New York: Penquin, 2004.

Celano, Peter. *To Live Is Christ: A 40-Day Journey with Saint Paul*. Brewster, Massachusetts: Paraclete Press, 2009.

Conners, Kenneth Wray. *Lord, Have You Got A Minute?* Valley Forge: Judson Press, 1979.

Connor, George, compiler. *Listening to Your Life: Daily Meditations with Frederick Buechner.* New York: Harper Collins, 1992.

Dossey, Larry. *Healing Words: The Power of Prayer and the Practice of Medicine.* San Francisco: Harper Collins Publisher, 1997.

Ferré, Nels F. S. *Strengthening the Spiritual Life.* New York: Harper & Row, 1951.

Forsyth, P. T. *The Soul of Prayer.* Grand Rapids, Michigan: William B. Eerdmans, 1916.

Fosdick, Harry Emerson. *The Meaning of Prayer.* New York: Association Press, 1929.

Foster, Richard J. *Celebration of Discipline.* San Francisco: Harper & Row, 1988.

_____. *Prayer: Finding the Heart's True Home.* San Francisco: Harper Collins, 1992.

Green, Thomas H. *Opening to God: A Guide to Prayer.* Indiana: Ava Maria Press, 2006.

Hall, Thor. *A Theology of Christian Devotion.* Nashville: The Upper Room, 1969.

Hanson, Bradley. *Teach Us to Pray.* Minneapolis: Augsburg, 1990.

Harkness, Georgia. *Disciplines of the Christian Life.* Richmond, Virginia: John Knox Press, 1967.

Harkness, Georgia. *Prayer and the Common Life.* New York: Abingdon Press, 1958.

Hinson, E. Glenn. *A Serious Call to a Contemplative Lifestyle, Revised Edition.* Macon, GA: Smyth & Helwys Publishing Company, 1993.

Hinson, E. Glenn. *The Reaffirmation of Prayer.* Nashville: Broadman Press, 1979.

Kelly, Thomas R. *A Testament of Devotion.* New York: Harper & Row, 1941.

Kelsey, Morton T. *The Other Side of Silence.* New York: Paulist Press, 1976.

Kepler, Thomas S. *Leaves from a Spiritual Notebook.* New York: Abingdon Press, 1960.

Killinger, John. *Bread for the Wilderness, Wine for the Journey.* Waco: Work Books, 1976.

_____. *The Cup and the Waterfall.* New York: Paulist Press, 1983.

_____. *Prayer: The Act of Being with God.* Waco, Word Press, 1981.

King, Jr., Martin Luther. *Strength of Love.* New York: Harper & Row, 1968.

Law, William. *A Serious Call to a Devout and Holy Life.* New York: E. P. Dutton, 1955.

Brother Lawrence. *The Practice of the Presence of God.* New York: Fleming H. Revell Co., 1895.

Lewis, C. S. Prayer: *Letters to Malcolm.* Glasgow: Harcourt, 2003.

Lewis, Edwin. *The Practice of the Christian Life.* Philadelphia: The Westminster Press, 1942.

Merton, Thomas. *New Seeds of Contemplation.* New York: New Directions Books, 1961.

Miley, Jeanie. *Ancient Psalms for Contemporary Pilgrims*. Macon, Georgia, Smyth & Helwys, 2003

_____. *Becoming Fire: Experience the Presence of Jesus Everyday*. Macon, Georgia: Smyth & Helwys, 2005.

_____. *Creative Silence*. Dallas: Word Publishing Co., 1989.

Miller, Samuel H. *Prayers for Daily Use*. Harpers & Brothers Publishers, 1957.

Niebuhr, Reinhold. *Justice and Mercy*. Louisville: Westminster/John Knox Press, 1974.

Novak, Michael. *Ascent to the Mountain, Flight of the Dove*. New York: Harper & Row, 1971.

Nouwen, Henri J. M. *The Way of the Heart*. New York: The Seabury Press, 1981.

O'Connor, Elizabeth. *Eighth Day of Creation*. Waco: Word Books, 1971.

_____. *Search for Silence*. Waco: Word Books, 1972.

Palmer, Parker J. *The Active Life*. San Francisco: Harper & Row, 1990.

Quoist, Michael. *Prayers*. New York: Avon, 1975.

_____. *With Open Heart*. New York: Crossroad, 1986.

Raines, Robert A. *Creative Brooding*. New York: Macmillian Co., 1966.

_____. *Soundings*. New York: Harper & Row, 1979.

Rauschenbusch, Walter. *Prayers of the Social Awakening*. Boston: The Pilgrim Press, 1910.

Rupp, Joyce. *May I Have This Dance*. Notre Dame, Indiana: Ave Maria Press, 1992.

Shawchuck, Norman and Rueben P. Job. *A Guide to Prayer for All Who Seek God*. Nashville: Upper Room, 2006.

Steere, Douglas. *On Beginning from Within*. New York: Harper & Brothers, 1943.

Swears, Thomas R. *The Approaching Sabbath: Spiritual Discipline for Pastors*. Nashville: Abingdon Press, 1991.

Taylor, Barbara Brown. *Mixed Blessings*. Cambridge, Massachusetts,: Cowley Publications, 1998.

The Confessions of St. Augustine. New York: E. P. Dutton, 1953.

Treatises and Sermons of Meister Eckhart. New York: Harper & Brothers, 1958.

Vestal, Daniel. *Being the Presence of Christ*. Nashville: Upper Room Books, 2008.

Warner, Hugh C. (compl.). *Daily Readings from William Temple*. New York: Abingdon Press, 1965.

Weatherhead, Leslie D. *A Private House of Prayer*. New York: Abingdon Press, 1958.

Willard, Dallas. *The Spirit of the Disciplines*. San Francisco: Harper & Collins, 1991.

Willimon, William H. *On A Wilde and Windy Mountain*. Nashville: Abingdon Press, 1984.

Wolpert, Daniel. *Creating a Life with God: The Call of Ancient Prayer Practices*. Nashville: Upper Room, 2005.

Wyon, Olive. *The School of Prayer*. London: SCM Press, 1957.

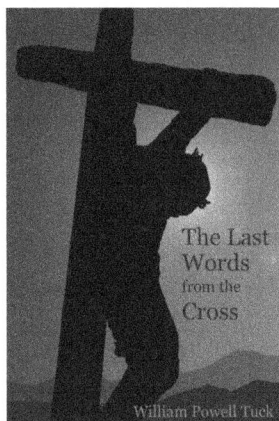

MORE FROM ENERGION PUBLICATIONS

Personal Study

The Jesus Paradigm	David Alan Black	$17.99
When People Speak for God	Henry Neufeld	$17.99
The Sacred Journey	Chris Surber	$11.99
The Spirit's Fruit	David Moffett-Moore	$9.99
Forgiveness	Harvey Brown, Jr.	$4.99

Christian Living

Faith in the Public Square	Robert D. Cornwall	$16.99
Grief: Finding the Candle of Light	Jody Neufeld	$8.99
Crossing the Street	Robert LaRochelle	$16.99
The Last Words from the Cross	William Powell Tuck	$9.99
My Life Story	Becky Lynn Black	$14.99

Bible Study

Learning and Living Scripture	Lentz/Neufeld	$12.99
From Inspiration to Understanding	Edward W. H. Vick	$24.99
Luke: A Participatory Study Guide	Geoffrey Lentz	$8.99
Philippians: A Participatory Study Guide	Bruce Epperly	$9.99
Ephesians: A Participatory Study Guide	Robert D. Cornwall	$9.99

Theology

Creation in Scripture	Herold Weiss	$12.99
Creation: the Christian Doctrine	Edward W. H. Vick	$12.99
Process Theology	Bruce G. Epperly	$4.99
Ultimate Allegiance	Robert D. Cornwall	$9.99
The Church Under the Cross	William Powell Tuck	$11.99
The Journey to the Undiscovered Country	William Powell Tuck	$9.99
Eschatology: A Participatory Study Guide	Edward W. H. Vick	$9.99

Ministry

Clergy Table Talk	Kent Ira Groff	$9.99
Wind and Whirlwind	David Moffett-Moore	$9.99

Generous Quantity Discounts Available

Dealer Inquiries Welcome

Energion Publications — P.O. Box 841

Gonzalez, FL_ 32560

Website: http://energionpubs.com

Phone: (850) 525-3916

www.ingramcontent.com/pod-product-compliance
Lightning Source LLC
Chambersburg PA
CBHW031557040426
42452CB00006B/333